Smile When They Call You Sleazy

Strategy & Encouragement for the Impact-Driven Entrepreneur

Written by Mary Cravets

For ordering information, special discount for bulk purchases, or to request Mary speak for your group, contact Mary through the contact page at www.MaryCravets.com.

ISBN: 978-1539352099

Dedication

This book is dedicated to my family. You are the reason I stay committed to the path of entrepreneurship.

To my parents, Fred and Gail Preller. You are the funniest, kindest people I'll ever know. Thank you. You have made everything in my life possible, in no small part because you didn't kill me during my teenage years.

Words fail me when it comes to my sister, Margaret Osako. Which I realize may not be a good way to start my book. You are my confidante, my friend, and I love you beyond all reason.

To my husband, Adam. You're my favorite. I love you to my soul, and nothing I've accomplished would have been possible without you.

Thank you to my mother- and father-in-law, Deb and Art Cravets. Your son is amazing. Thank you for raising him right, and for loving me as a part of your family, even though we had a rocky start.

Last but not least, to my nieces Hannah and Zoe, and my nephew Owen, thank you. You inspire me with your brilliance and weirdness. Keep being true to yourself, no matter what. And when you're ready to start your own business, call Auntie Mary and we'll do it right.

Table of Contents

Chapter 4: An Entrepreneur Walks into a Dentist's Office

Chapter 5: Imaginary Obstacles

Chapter 6: Ditch the Deposits and Go to Vegas

Introduction

"Timing, perseverance, and ten years of trying will eventually make you look like an overnight success."
- Biz Stone, co-founder of Twitter

Wow! The co-founder of Twitter?

From him, those "ten years of trying," sound almost romantic and heroic, don't they? **He fought the good fight and came out a champion, even when everyone thought he was crazy.**

But what about those ten crazy years? Can you imagine quotes from that time?

> "I have just enough money in my checking account to cover the month, with no idea what to do next."

> "In one day, I got a new client **and** a deal fell through. It feels like I'm just spinning my wheels."

> "My spouse asked me for the third time this month why I'm crying over my business when I could just go get a job."

> "I work and work to make a positive impact in the lives of others and I just got called 'sleazy' on Facebook."

I made these up. Because who would be crazy enough to write about the grueling days of entrepreneurship?

This girl.

All through my toughest years of entrepreneurship, I wrote and I wrote. I laid bare every struggle, every strategy, every mindset shift I had to make in order to persevere long enough to become an "overnight success".

I put everything down on paper that helped me build a business, to stretch my comfort zone, and to laugh at the absurdity of entrepreneurship.

You've heard the quote, "Entrepreneurs are the only people who will work 80 hours a week for themselves to avoid working 40 hours a week for someone else."

Absurd, right?

But also incomplete.

Entrepreneurs, especially those who are Impact-Driven, work those crazy hours and endure the struggle because we are committed to making a difference. We improve the lives of others. We educate. We inspire. We transform.

If you are here to make an impact while making a living, this book will help you laugh and be inspired and focus your efforts. It will let you know that you are not alone on this crazy journey.

And who knows? Maybe it could even help you shave a few years off of *your* journey to "overnight success".

I believe in you.

Mary Cravets

Chapter 1

Smile When They Call You Sleazy

Encouragement & Inspiration

Smile When They Call You Sleazy

Here's one thing they don't tell you when you start a business: You will be criticized.

You'll be criticized by well-meaning friends and family who don't want to see you hurt or disappointed.

You'll be criticized by competitors who want you to stay out of the game so they don't feel threatened.

Worst of all, you'll be criticized by random strangers who don't know you, but think you should be playing by their rules, not yours.

It is tough some days, I won't lie. And although I personally have developed a thicker skin over the years, criticism still hurts.

Like when I was called "sleazy" recently, I got a sick feeling in my stomach. But after a few minutes of hurt and worry, I smiled.

Because I know from past experience, **criticism is a herald of good things to come.**

Here's the routine I've built for dealing with critics:

Have compassion. Critics are afraid: afraid to hope, afraid to fail, afraid to get screwed over, afraid of success... and the list goes on forever. When people take shots at you, they are simply scared. Be graceful, be kind, be understanding. Then let them go and move on.

Center yourself. When criticism throws you for a loop, get clear about why you do what you do. It's all about making a positive impact. A positive impact on your family, your finances, your freedom and on others. When you re-center yourself on your vision and what is most important to you, the force of criticism diminishes significantly.

Have a sense of humor. Because, let's face it, the life of the entrepreneur is pretty hilarious. We'll work 60 hours a week for a roller-coaster income in order to be "free" from a 40-hour a week job with a steady paycheck. People who criticize are often hitting a nerve we've be unable to laugh at (yet). Take yourself too seriously, and criticism can destroy you.

Look for the opportunity. Ask yourself, "Is there any truth to this criticism? What can I learn from this? Is it simply to persevere with grace? Or, is there something good that can come of this? A blog? A book title?" Don't change everything in response to criticism…that's the worst thing you can do. But the second worst thing is to refuse to be open to the opportunities it offers.

Know good things are on their way. When criticism comes, a growth spurt generally follows. Criticism is kind of like a test. It's the energy of Entrepreneurship tapping you on the shoulder and whispering to you, "It's rough out there, and people will push your buttons and pull you down when they get the chance. Do you have what it takes? Are you willing to take the abuse with the rewards?" In my career it took about 5 years of ups and downs (and pity parties when someone threw rotten tomatoes) to recognize this pattern, but it has held true time and time again.

So, when someone calls you pushy or greedy or too big for your britches or sleazy…just smile. Be kind and laugh. Recommit to your vision, look for the opportunity and believe, down to your toes, that good things are coming your way.

Am I Getting Ahead if I'm Going Backwards?

In the wonderful worlds of personal growth and entrepreneurism, the answer to that question is often YES.

Progress towards a goal is generally thought of as a linear process… but in reality, it rarely is. It's no wonder we get frustrated!

It's important to understand that progress and direction do not always run together. This came into sharp focus when I heard a story told by the woman who led the first American Women's Mount Everest Expedition.

She explained that when climbing Mount Everest, you can't go directly from base camp to the summit. In fact, you spend the bulk of your time going *backwards* to regroup in order to make the next ascent.

Look at the climb process:

- Base Camp (17,600 ft.), spend a few days to acclimatize
- Set out for Camp 1 (19,900 ft.).
- Go back to Base Camp
- Head to Camp 2 (21,300 ft.)
- Go all the way back to Base Camp
- Climb up through the camps again to the summit.

If they didn't go backwards as a part of the process, climbers would not adjust to the altitude or build the stamina necessary to survive reaching the summit.

If you feel like you're on a detour on the path to your goals, pause and reflect. Are you "adjusting to the altitude", so to speak, by learning perseverance or patience? Are you meeting new people who might help you along your way? Trust the process.

Whatever the lesson, know that going backwards is a natural part of progress. Be open to what you're learning, be gentle with yourself, and enjoy the climb!

Mind the Gap

I work with smart, driven people who are constantly growing themselves and their businesses.

I also happen to BE one of those people.

Our natural state seems to be one of mild to severe dissatisfaction. We constantly ask ourselves, "What are we missing? Who is ahead of us? What's the next opportunity?"

What would you call this? Greed? Lack of gratitude? Insanity?

Personally, I call it the natural mental environment brought on and sustained by entrepreneurship.

Here are a few simple truths about working for yourself, and some do's and don'ts to help you survive them.

There is always more to learn.
DO implement your current knowledge. The BEST ideas are not theoretical, they are the ones that are put into action.
DON'T drown yourself in so much learning that you avoid implementing.

There is always someone doing better than you.
DO recognize yourself for what you're doing great, and learn from those ahead of you.
DON'T paralyze yourself with comparisons.

As long as you're an entrepreneur, you live in the gap between where you are and where you want to be.

DO find ways to be conscious of that gap, and co-exist with it peacefully.

DON'T define that gap as evidence that you are wrong, broken or less than anyone else.

Hmmm... Was That an Over-share?

You'll come to learn that I tend to just say whatever is on my mind, and also write about it with abandon. You may already be asking yourself, "Mary, why do you over-share all the crazy stuff you think about? Don't you want to be seen as some kind of stable, sane expert?"

So before you start questioning your **own** sanity for actually reading my stuff, I thought it best to let you know why I intentionally choose to be blissfully transparent.

Many years ago, I started my own business, and discovered that entrepreneurship required personal growth. As I started down the road of self-improvement, I took note of all of the incredibly successful teachers, and I made some very destructive assumptions.

I assumed these teachers were all constantly happy, health-nut, marathon-running millionaires. In short, I assumed that they never had a bad day.

Why was this assumption so destructive?

Because if I ever had a bad day, or ate a doughnut, or experienced failure, or – God forbid – was simply lazy for a day, I thought that it meant I would never succeed.

Then one day, I listened to a lecture given by a wildly successful business owner. While recounting a story, he casually mentioned that a few weeks ago he had had a really bad day.

WHAT?!

A light went on for me – "You mean you can have bad days and still be successful?"

I wish I could say that I was more sophisticated when I started my own business, but the fact is, until that moment, I hadn't realized that I'd made those assumptions. But they affected me subconsciously every single day.

I am so thankful to this businessman for his honesty and authenticity. My hope is that my blissful transparency – about both the successes and the insanity – will help others have the critical "ah-ha" moments they need to succeed faster.

Lazy Successes

I am a very driven person. I actually love working, and believe the harder I work, the more results I'll get.

Flash back to a few years ago when I had a series of minor maladies. Things like a really annoying irritation going in my left eye that felt like I had sand or an eyelash in it all the time. It wasn't painful or life-threatening, just an aggravating distraction.

As a result, I seriously did NOT want to work. At all. I ended up doing just the bare minimum for a few weeks. But the weird thing was that I got more results – people joining my programs, more clients, and new events. Puzzling.

Upon reflection, I can think of three reasons why this happened:

1. I focused on getting only the essentials done, and left the "fluff" behind.
2. I said "no" to taking on new things.
3. I relaxed and took care of myself.

The challenge? Remembering to put these habits in place **before** exhaustion or illness set in!

One Foot on the Gas and One on the Brake

I visited my husband at his office, and I saw a woman walking across the parking lot lugging a box of stuff toward the nearby coffee shop. She was in her 50s or 60s and had a tired air about her, yet fluidity to her walk - almost a carelessness to it.

Something itched at the back of my mind; what was this quality I was witnessing?

Then it hit me – she's an entrepreneur!

I saw a beautiful stubbornness that I related to without her having to utter a word: the absolute commitment to do ANYTHING in order to avoid being tied down to working for someone else.

Soul sister!

I have a special place in my heart for entrepreneurs, especially those who are taking their first wobbly steps towards working for themselves. I sigh with almost motherly pride when I see an entrepreneur set up an information table at a coffee shop, or in front of the health food store. My heart aches with joy when I see a man at a restaurant present his "30 second commercial" to his waiter.

It makes me laugh – the inexperience, the tenacity, the enthusiasm – it's all just such a strange and wonderful combination. We put our pride, our hearts and our hopes on the line in pursuit of freedom.

And yes, I realize I am romanticizing. Along with my sighing and the aching, I know the shadow side. Sleepless nights from both success highs and failure lows. The ups and downs of income. The skepticism of family and friends who think we are completely nuts. On the down days, we suspect they might be right.

It's no wonder entrepreneurs often feel like they have one foot on the gas and one on the brake.

How do you manage this sometimes gear-grinding feeling? Stay focused on taking action. Stay beautiful. Stay stubborn.

Some Big Shoes to Fill

In 2013, I stepped out onto a much bigger stage. It was an incredibly successful, dynamic, go-go-go year in my business where I tripled my income and grew tremendously on a personal level.

It was exhilarating and nerve-wracking in equal measure. I often caught my internal and external realities at odds. Kind of like my insides would look at the chances I was taking in the outside world, and worriedly whisper in my ear, "WOW, those are some big shoes to fill... are you sure they're mine?"

At the end of the year and with 2014 just around the corner, I felt like I needed some kind of ritual to fully incorporate the bolder reality I created in 2013. As it turned out, life had this well in hand for me.

Over the holidays spent with family, my sister and I snuck out of the house to do a little shopping.

After hitting the gourmet coffee shop (guilty pleasure #1) and an ultimate beauty supply store (guilty pleasure #2), we went to the designer shoe mega-store (guilty pleasure #3). Row upon row of shoes – bliss!

Scouring the aisles for the perfect black boots, I found many contenders, and rejected others because they didn't have my size. Nothing in my size was right. Then I went back to one especially promising pair that wasn't available in my size, and thought, "I'll just try a half size bigger."

Lo and behold, they fit!

Now with my 40th birthday a few years in my rearview mirror, you might suggest that this size increase is due to gravity, fallen arches, or some other age-related factor. But this is my story, so I'm going to ignore reality and opt for a prettier metaphor.

Those big shoes I created last year? The ones I thought maybe I was just borrowing?

They are all mine. I've stepped into them. I wear them. I own them.

Being RIGHT in the Express Lane

I was at the grocery store the other day, and was feeling really rushed. I had just picked up food for the evening's event, and felt like I was cutting it really close with timing.

After estimating the number of items in my cart, I dashed to the "15 Items or Less" check-out stand. With only one person ahead of me, and no one looking like they were going to file in behind, I figured this was the best way to get out of there in a hurry.

As I unloaded my cart, a man joined the line behind me. He had a hand basket with just two items in it. He surveyed my load of groceries, and assumed an expression of supreme exasperation.

So what did I do? I treated him like I treat everyone. I smiled and said hello.

He sighed loudly, pointedly looked at the sign that indicated the grocery item limit, and under his breath muttered, "Hmm… wish some people knew how to count."

Oh boy do I hate conflict… but for some reason this situation immediately struck me as funny.

I looked at him, and then looked at my items (which I still hadn't counted), and said, "I didn't count, did I?" I counted up my items and came up with 17. Whoops! Call the grocery police!

Smiling, despite my worry about being late, I said to the man, "I'm 2 items over, would you like to go ahead of me?"

Here's the punch line: he said NO.

At that point, it took every ounce of restraint not to laugh out loud. Lest you feel sorry for this man, understand that I felt like laughing, not just because of the situation at hand, but also because I wanted to laugh at myself.

It was like looking in a mirror.

The situation fully embodied a phrase a mentor of mine challenged me with over and over: "Do you want to be right, or do you want to have peace?"

I can think of so many times in my life when I was given a way out of a frustrating situation, but rather than allowing myself to experience relief, I chose a stance of self righteousness. Because I was RIGHT, damn it!!!

This poor guy, I truly meant him no harm. He had no idea what was in my heart that day, and he has no idea that, in an odd way, he uplifted me. I left the store that day with my shopping cart, ran a few steps with it, and then rode it like a scooter to my car, thinking, "I CHOOSE PEACE!"

It's Not JUST About the Mercedes

I hear a lot of positive-thinking teachers preach, "Just create the perfect vision of your goal, and the 'how' will take care of itself."

Well… not exactly.

My delightful imagination helped clarify my line of thinking by providing scenarios of two people achieving the same goal of getting a brand new Mercedes:

Scenario #1: A woman wrestles herself out of a brand new black Mercedes. She is on the phone, frowning, juggling her keys and purse and at the same time trying to look at something on her iPad. She is disheveled, tired, anxious, and she's running late. In other words – she's a hot mess.

Scenario #2: A woman swings herself out of a brand new black Mercedes. She grabs her purse with a smile on her face and heads off with a spring in her step. She looks put-together and comfortable. She's happy, satisfied, and well-rested.

Both women got the Mercedes, but only one is thoroughly enjoying it and her life in general. The difference between being refreshed or exhausted when we reach our goals is how we get there. Do you struggle, worry, avoid, get distracted, and overwork? Or do you plan, implement, evaluate, and enjoy?

The "how" matters, and with a little attention, can be just as fulfilling as the goal.

When Success Gets Personal

Did you know that 87% of statistics are made up on the spot? With that disclaimer out of the way, I shall proceed...

A friend of mine teaches classes at a massage school. She's been teaching classes for years and years, and recently got one poor evaluation from one student. She was NOT a happy camper.

And I could relate, because the more people I meet, and the more events I do, the more feedback I get – both positive and negative. The negative always seems more powerful.

With the hopes of providing a little perspective, I shared with her a statistic I made up to help me deal with some of the negativity. It goes like this: If you are doing your work with integrity:

- 5% of all people are going to not like you – that's just the way it goes.
- When you know 100 people, that percentage equals 5 people. When you have access to 1000 people, that's 50 people. When you get exposure to 2000 people, that's 100 people.
- Realize that even though the number changes, the percentage doesn't, so accept it.

As you are succeeding, expanding your reach, and increasing your exposure, it's very likely that more people will not like you. But remember…

- For every 5 who don't like you, 95 appreciate you. Listen to them instead.
- People who have few successes have very few critics.
- Critics can be our best teachers. Remember to not cast them in the role of the villain: learn what you can from them, treat them with respect, and let them go.

Even though my statistic is 96.7% fictional, I hope you get the point!

Inspiration from "What Not to Wear"

Years ago, my sister got me hooked on the TV show "What Not to Wear". If you're not familiar with the premise, two fabulous New York stylists help women ditch their frumpy, inappropriate, or outdated wardrobes, and not only overhaul their closet, but also confront issues of self-esteem and body image.

This show is junk food for the mind, and I watch it to unplug. But without meaning to, it provided me with a moment of inspiration.

In every episode, the hosts review the guest's wardrobe and proceed to throw away every article of clothing in it. It's often quite emotional for the guest to let go of their familiar yet ill-fitting clothes. In one episode, the hosts asked their guest if she was having a hard time with this process of letting go, to which she replied, **"I guess you can't get something better if your hands are full of something else."**

I found this image so clarifying: hands full of some grubby old sweatshirt, safe and familiar, but ultimately no longer in alignment with who she is and what she wants.

As you grow as an entrepreneur, remember to constantly be rooting out your own version of the cruddy sweatshirt. Make room for something truly stunning!

Chapter 2

Tell Me What You CAN Do

Taking Action

Tell Me What You CAN Do

A few years ago, I was listening to a client complain, "I don't have time to do this. I don't have time to do that..."

We'd been having this conversation for months, and in frustration I burst out, "I'm not interested in what you can't do, tell me what you CAN do!"

Not the most elegant delivery, I'll admit, but my point hit home. As a result of that outburst, my client profoundly shifted the way she managed her business and her life. We identified the inner voice that silently kept her stuck in paralyzing inaction.

So what are you focusing on: the problem or the solution?

Now before I am accused of being one of those annoying "just think positive and bury your head in the sand if anything negative comes your way" types, let me clarify. I'm not talking about being happy-happy all the time, I'm talking about learning to direct your thinking to be in alignment with what you **want**, rather than what you **don't** want.

Now that I've given my disclaimer...

Here's an example of how directing your thinking can free you:

> **Current Perspective:** *I'm busy from 8 to 9, 10 to 11:30 and 2:30 to 5*
> By focusing on the busy time, you're giving yourself messages that you are busy, there is not enough

time, and you'll get nothing accomplished. This subconscious belief directs your actions and becomes self-fulfilling and you're likely to get nothing accomplished. With this perspective, you're convincing yourself that you have no time at all.

Simple Alternative: *I have time available from 9 to 10, and 11:30 to 2:30*
Now you're giving yourself the opportunity to see the time that was completely invisible to you before. Without rearranging a single appointment, suddenly four hours just opened up!

This perspective shift can be used on any belief based in "can't", "don't have" and "not enough". Use it to free you from money issues, doubts about your own abilities or any perceived lack of resources.

Clarity and My Deep, Dark Secret

Yesterday I received an email from a friend I made more than 20 years ago. She was updating our whole group about how she was doing in Canada.

I replied back and joked how the year we spent together probably caused my back problems. And it got me thinking…

You see, when I was traveling with this group, we carried around 23 tons of stage equipment. Lights, sound, sets – you name it. It was a huge production, and here's the kicker – we were also our own roadies. 100 twenty-somethings, setting up at 2pm and striking the set at 11pm again and again across the US, Canada, Mexico and Australia.

As I wrote to my friend I recalled how I hated setting up and taking down the set. No surprise, right? But what I also remembered is that I took a turn on "truck crew".

This was the toughest job. Helping everyone work together, getting things out in the right order, and then – after a full day of set up, rehearsal, community service and performing – making it all fit back into the truck.

Working on the truck crew was physically harder, but for some reason it seemed easier than randomly carting things off the truck and setting up sound one day, lights the next, speaker stacks the next, risers the next.

Why do I think it was easier? It's because I had a specific, clearly defined role and a specific, clearly defined goal. I knew where to be, what was expected, and what the end result should look like. The organized heavy lifting was easy compared to the chaotic lighter work.

Can you relate? Work becomes so much easier when you know where you are going, and what is expected of you.

You got the moral of the story, so now I bet you want to know my deep dark secret. Here it is…

The group I traveled with is the international performing and service group (often maligned on the David Letterman Show and parodied on The Simpsons), Up With People.

No, I will NOT sing the theme song for you.

Got a Case of "It's All Been Done"?

Have you ever been visited by this sneaky saboteur? The "it's all been done" syndrome?

I had a case of it recently as I wracked my brain for a topic to write an article about. Every time I came up with an idea, I immediately told myself, "yeah, but that's been done before," and it kept me spinning for days.

After giving up for the fifth time, I was reminded of a moment of profound change I experienced many years ago. I was on a teleclass about professional speaking taught by an industry giant. I chose to be on the call because I LOVE public speaking, but I always held myself back because I couldn't come up with a 100% unique topic to speak on.

Giving voice to my fears, the teacher acknowledged that there are very few speakers with wholly original ideas. But then he said, "You can't let that stop you. **There are people out there who can only hear your voice."**

Boom.

I knew exactly what he meant. I'd hear a concept from five different people, but only fully absorb it from the one person whose "voice" – energy, experience, persona, attitude, philosophy – I truly connected with.

I work with business owners all the time who hide their talents, insights, and services because of this feeling of "it's been done" or "everyone else is doing the same thing."

Don't let this sabotage you, and do not use it as an excuse to not pursue your life's work. There are people out there who are listening for your voice. It's time to speak up!

Consistency: The Most Misunderstood Key to Success

Consistency is a critical key to success. Intellectually we know this, but putting it into practice can be a constant battle. And why is that?

Because consistency has a plodding, dreadfully dull quality to it, doesn't it? And freedom-loving entrepreneurs tend to resist anything that resembles the regular schedule of employment... but it doesn't have to be that way!

Consistency – done right – frees up your time, energizes you, and gives you results.

Here are three tips to give you a new perspective on consistency:

1. **Structure your consistency on a larger scale.** Entrepreneurs start businesses to free themselves from a 9 to 5 schedule – so is it any surprise that you're bored and resistant to a day-in, day-out rote version of consistency? Instead of having daily tasks, consider tackling them on a weekly or monthly basis. I consistently do the majority of my marketing each month in just one or two days – often in just a few hours on the last few days of the month. If I had to do my tasks a few at a time each day, I'd go crazy.
2. **Build variety into your consistency.** Most entrepreneurs I know crave new experiences, so variety is key. Here are a few examples of variety paired with consistency: be consistent about

networking, but attend a variety of different events; be consistent about touching base with past customers, but vary how you contact them (email, mail, social media, phone); be consistent about email marketing, but send a variety of tips, videos and photos. Variety keeps you engaged, and helps you avoid falling victim to distraction.

3. **Evaluate your consistency... consistently.** Even if you've scheduled your consistency to give you freedom and structured it to give you variety, if you aren't seeing results, you'll just be consistently busy with nothing to show for your efforts. To counteract this, simply track your actions and evaluate your results, then be quick to adjust them when needed.

Change your perspective on consistency and then implement your new perspective. Instead of being bored, distracted, and unmotivated, you will be engaged, focused, energized – and seeing results!

Determine, Engage, Ignore

You have no control over the state of the country's economy, or someone saying no to you, or whether or not people return your phone calls.

So stop focusing on those things. You'll just make yourself crazy.

Focus on what you DO have control over. Things like making phone calls, writing articles, sending emails, asking for business, attending networking functions. All of these things are 100% within your control.

Keeping this focus in mind, here are three simple steps to make your business activities more effective, easy and profitable.

1. **Determine which activities (the ones you have 100% control over) lead to the results you want.** Look over your newest 10 clients, and determine which activities led them to your door. Do you see a trend between making phone calls and receiving referrals? Sending an e-newsletter and making sales? Focus on the activities that bring results.

2. **Engage in these activities consistently.** Decide how many times you'll engage in these activities, and do them consistently. For instance, when I was in real estate, my activities were: 1 mailing to my database per month, 1 client lunch per week, 5 phone calls per day, and sending 3 note cards per day. This consistent activity led me to triple my business in one year.

3. **Ignore the stuff that is beyond your control.** It's almost like you have to put blinders on to block out the loud, insistent negativity and fear that comes with all of the things that are beyond your control. But you must do it if you don't want to go crazy!

Now guess what happens when you decide, engage, and ignore?

- You feel more relaxed, knowing you're investing in the highest return on investment activities
- You have more time in your day
- New clients seems to come out of nowhere

Sounds too easy, right? There is a rampant belief that in order to be effective, a solution must be complicated. Nothing could be further from the truth. Focus on what works. Ignore the rest.

That is all.

The Worst Thing About Mountain Climbing

As I was prioritizing my to-do list one evening, a random thought popped into my head. It went something like this:

"You know the WORST thing about mountain climbing? The hardest part is at the end! Think about it. Just before you get to the top where you're facing the steepest part, you have less energy than at any other time during the climb."

Bizarre, right? I shrugged it off and prioritized my list like this:

1. Pay cell phone bill
2. Add sponsors to web site
3. Schedule my week
4. Clear off my desk

Another thought then scampered through my consciousness: "Do them backwards." I thought – ok little voice, you got it.

I added "do them backwards" to my list, and went to bed.

I woke up the next day and took my advice, just to see what would happen. Instead of doing the small tasks right away, I took on the bigger tasks first to take advantage of my focus and energy then saved the smaller tasks for later when my energy flagged.

And surprise, surprise, it was so much easier.

Do the hardest tasks first, when you're refreshed and full of energy, and you will build momentum throughout your day. It's much easier than dealing with an ever more challenging mountain of work.

Ahh... That's a Little Better

One day as I was heading out to the store I thought, "I'll take my vitamins later." Which really meant, "I won't take my vitamins today."

Then the gentle question popped into my head, "Can I do this a little better?"

The answer, of course, was simple: take the vitamins now.

What a great question to help stay on the path of continuous improvement without getting overwhelmed. So simple. Almost too simple to be taken seriously.

Because it's easy to dismiss such a small step, isn't it? In the moment, "a little better" seems insignificant. What is walking an extra 5 minutes going to do? What is adding vegetables going to get me? How is calling one more client going to change my income? Why should I be kind to the grocery clerk?

We want instant gratification, and adopting the habit of "a little better" does not feed that need. Instead, results come gradually over time. Walking a little more allows you to move more freely, and keep up with kids or grandkids. Eating veggies can keep you healthier later in life. Calling your clients can build a support team of raving fans who make your business operate like a well-oiled machine because they consistently refer to you. Being kind lifts up everyone around you.

When you look to do just a little better in every situation, your actions are not dramatic, but in the end, the results ARE revolutionary.

So keep the phrase in mind – "Can I do this a little better?" Walk for 5 more minutes. Eat extra veggies. Call one more client. Offer a kind word when none is required.

Reach Any Goal in 3 Steps

Many years ago I noticed my clothes were a bit tight, and it occurred to me that I never really got back into the swing of healthy eating after the previous Christmas.

So I started the battle to re-establish my healthy habits. I got back to eating right and exercising, but then fell off the wagon for my birthday. I got back into the swing of things, and finally, after many failed attempts, I got into the routine where exercising and eating right felt normal, rather than a struggle.

Then one short week after the commitment really took hold, I hopped on the scale. Prepared to be dazzled by my progress, I quickly discovered I'd dropped only .6 pounds. My mind started racing, "Should I cut back more? Exercise more? No fruit? Eat more at lunch and less at breakfast? What should I change to reach my goal? I've been doing everything right, what's the point?"

All of a sudden I felt like I was talking to my clients who, just because they had a bad week in business, want to start changing everything.

The parallels are striking, and whether you want to fit into your skinny jeans or reach a big business goal, here are 3 simple steps that will help:

1. **Get clear.** Set a goal and make a decision to work towards it.
2. **Get a plan.** Define the steps necessary to reach your goal.
3. **Get into action.** Execute your plan consistently, track your results, and adjust as needed.

You'll know you've missed one of these steps if you're constantly overworking, reinventing, and everything feels difficult. If you have these steps in place, but you're constantly looking for new opportunities and feeling hopeless and impatient, you're not giving enough time for the steps to produce results.

Whatever your goal, when these steps are in place, your progress is consistent, and you experience a profound sense of ease and accomplishment.

So even though it's challenging in the hustle and bustle of everyday life, take the time to get your plan together. Then go out there and do it. Stop driving yourself crazy trying every new fad out there. Business, and life, is so much easier if you just take a little time to step back and evaluate.

Off Course

"How did I get so far off course?"

I get asked this question a lot. And the answer is – drift.

Drift is subtle. It happens when you set your actions along a path that is just a few degrees off course from your goals. But those few degrees off course, if we compare it to a physical map, can be the difference between ending up in Disneyland, and say, Montana.

And the worst part about drift? You don't even notice that it's happening.

How do you know you're drifting? You're in the midst of drift if you're saying things like, "Where am I?", "Why isn't this working?", "How did I get here?", or "It's going to take me forever to get back on track."

How do you get back on course? To get back on track, review your business and look at the times when you were getting the results you wanted. Track those results back to the activities that got you there, and start doing those things on a consistent basis.

How do you counteract drift? To stay on track, stay consistent with your activity, track your results, evaluate, and adjust your course.

And hire someone to help you stay accountable.

Having someone help you stay aware of the tendency to

drift, and counteract it consistently, is one of the most important things you will do in your business. It will save you time, sanity, and a whole lot of money.

I Didn't Want to Write This

On a Tuesday several years ago, I scheduled time to write an article. It was the first item on my list, but all I could do was sit there and stare at my computer. Nothing was coming to me. I started fiddling around with email, looking at old articles, going on Facebook...and before I knew it, the day was almost gone. I hadn't written the article, and because I was stuck on the idea that it MUST be done first, little else on my list was accomplished. Add to the mix my feelings of failure and frustration, and I had a recipe for an all-around bummer of a day.

The lesson? Keep your priorities in order, but if something isn't working, move on, rather than losing your momentum.

In that same article-writing instance, as I was down to the wire before the deadline, I found myself thinking, "Well, I'm not inspired to write, so maybe I'll work on something else for a little while." That's valid, right? Because I'm not INSPIRED. But the fact is, writing articles on a consistent basis is an integral part of my business plan. So I muscled my way through it, keeping my eye on my priorities.

The lesson? You can't be inspired all the time, so sometimes you need to push through and do what MUST be done.

The process of article writing has been a great teacher. I am forever getting writing ideas from the day-to-day happenings in my life (see current article). One thing I've learned the hard way is that when the mood to write strikes, I MUST drop everything and write. This habit was developed out of sheer frustration from being too strict of a time manager.

For instance, I'd be working on a task and suddenly come up with a great idea for an article. In the past, I'd stick to my guns and keep working on the task at hand, trusting that I'd remember the idea and write the article later. But that never happened. Many "aha" moments of inspiration were lost forever.

The lesson? If you're in the middle of something, and suddenly find yourself motivated to do a task that you generally find challenging - take advantage of the moment and do it!

Do you find some of these lessons contradictory? Yep – welcome to life! This is the challenge: knowing when to use each lesson. Am I inspired to write or avoiding my accounting? Am I appropriately muscling through an article or am I pushing too hard and coming up with garbage? Am I moving on to keep my momentum or dodging a necessary task?

Look at Your Feet

During an unusually stressful week, I took time to clear my head with a hike in Sedona. As I walked, I glanced down at my feet, and it brought to mind a common question I get asked by clients – "How can I be sure I'm on the right path?"

My answer? **Look at your feet.** Trust me, this works whether you look at it philosophically or practically.

Philosophically: Personally, I believe that we have purpose in life, and that it is impossible for us to be on the wrong path. Look at your feet, and they will always show you exactly where you're "supposed" to be.

Practically: Even if you don't agree with my philosophy, look at your feet for a practical perspective. If you're questioning your path, any change in direction must start from precisely where you are right now.

Chapter 3

Pondering My Sanity

Struggle and Stress

Pondering My Sanity

At one point in my career, I had to make some tough decisions about a successful networking event I had created. I was a stress case – literally going through crying jags and paralyzing fear for weeks.

Time passed and I found myself calmly rolling out the new guidelines for event coordinators and event fees, and the unbidden thought ran through my head, "This is so simple and straightforward."

WHAT?! Weeks of stress and then I suddenly accepted that my natural state is to think the changes I lost sleep over are the most obvious and easy things in the world? I started to wonder if I was actually a crazy person barely passing as sane.

In the midst of pondering my sanity, I listened to a teleclass by a brilliant coach where she introduced the idea of creating internal tension (but never external pressure) to get people to move forward. She distinguished the difference between internal pressure (tension) and external pressure (stress).

How I wished I had learned these ideas before my weeks of paralyzing fear.

I could have, in the midst of the pressure I was feeling, taken a step back and asked myself, "Is this tension or stress?"

Tension is an indicator of growth. It arises when there is a conflict between old ideas and new, past habits and future possibilities. It arises from searching for change, and being on the cusp of finding it.

And stress? It arises when there is an outside threat. This may be an actual physical threat, but more often in the business world, it's a threat in the form of overloading yourself; saying yes when you want to say no, or not having a clear plan to achieve your goals.

Building the strength of focus to be able to stop and evaluate a stressful situation is one of the most important habits I've learned as an entrepreneur. Because when you back off of tension, you lose momentum in your business. And when you keep going under stress, you burn out.

But truth be told, it's no easy task to tell the difference between the two in a high-pressure moment. In my opinion, they feel exactly the same.

When feeling under pressure, your best bet is to pause, take a deep breath, and ask, "Is this something I need to let go of because it's useless fear and pressure (stress) or is this something I need to lean in to because I'm just experiencing the discomfort that comes with learning and growing (tension)?"

Seven Strategies to Manage Business Stress

1. Find ways to make other people smile. I read a novel in which a character said, "Winning makes you feel great. Helping someone else win makes you feel great, longer." Helping others gets you out of your own stress.

2. Create standards. Standards put your priorities into practical application on a daily basis. In other words, they let you design your life. For instance, my standards include a definition of an ideal client, a minimum number of yoga classes per week and a maximum number of caffeinated beverages per day. Your list may also include specific business activities, such as a number of phone calls to clients or daily prospecting activity.

3. Address "nags" promptly. If there are things in your life that are nagging at you, such as bad news you have to break, or even just purchases waiting to be exchanged, take care of them. These little nagging tasks are incredibly draining and reduce your ability to deal with normal stresses.

4. Create systems. Creating systems - written step-by-step processes - reduces stress in two ways. First, it allows you to complete tasks without spending a lot of mental energy figuring them out each time. And second, when it's time to delegate the task, you spend less time explaining it to your assistant. This ties in directly to the next strategy.

5. Delegate. My guideline for delegation is simple: If it doesn't require your personality or expertise, do everything you can to delegate it. Delegate your data entry and bookkeeping, and see if you don't feel twenty pounds lighter! For most people, delegating does not come naturally, but it is absolutely worth it!

6. Go easy on yourself. Every single person I know, including me, is harder on themselves than on any other person in their lives. Accomplishments we'd congratulate others for, we judge as not good enough in ourselves. Give yourself a pat on the back for all of the great things you do.

7. Let it out, carefully. Don't keep everything inside, but be selective who you confide in. Go to people you know will sympathize, but who will also encourage you to move beyond the stress, and into solutions.

Don't Get Crazy Hungry

A while ago, I bought a pair of dress pants in a size larger than the rest of my clothes; just needed some breathing room around the beltline, if you know what I mean. Two months later, I noticed I had **outgrown** those pants, along with every other pair I owned.

As much as I wanted to believe it was a growth spurt, and supermodel height was in my near future, I had to face the fact it was time to change my eating habits.

So I began eating right, and being really restrictive with what I ate. A month passed and I barely saw any results. Then all of a sudden, it seemed like every day I saw the scale moving in the right direction. I was puzzled – what had changed?

Very quickly I realized I had done just one simple thing – I stopped letting myself get crazy hungry. That's it.

When I got really hungry, my body felt deprived and panicky and held on to my extra weight to store up against an impending famine. By consistently nourishing myself with foods on my approved eating plan, my body realized it wouldn't be starved or made to suffer. No need to hold on to the fat stores in case of emergency!

When I fleshed out (so to speak) this theory, business parallels became immediately apparent. Think about it…

When you consistently do the things that feed your business, do you stress out? Do you gorge yourself on self-pity? Are you bloated with worry? Do your goals seem to be moving further away from you? Nope.

So how do you keep from feeling crazy hungry in business?

1. Identify the activities that best nourish your business.
2. Engage in those "nourishing" activities consistently.
3. Write down your goals.
4. Track your activity and progress.
5. Evaluate your results, and adjust your activity as needed.

Keep your business nourished, and you will keep those feelings of panic and stress at bay.

Confession Time

I found a new solution to stress: Confession. The particular stress I used my new solution on was made up of equal parts frenzy, pretending everything was ok, and confusion.

You see, there was a project I was working on, and if it didn't go well, I wouldn't meet an obligation I made to some colleagues. A terrible feeling.

So I had been running around with a crazy smile on my face saying "It's ok! No worries!" When in fact, things were not ok, and I was stressed out.

What did I do? I confessed. I laid out the situation to my colleagues and let them know I would understand if they wanted to bow out of their commitment.

In an instant, 95 % of my stress was gone. Of course, it got me thinking...what happened exactly?x

My stress was caused by getting further and further out of alignment with my integrity. By simply telling the truth, I snapped back into alignment. Right away, new ideas flowed in and I felt my energy return.

Here are some ways to know when it might be time to 'fess up:

- When you're telling yourself, "I'm doing everything I can!" Are you really? Or are you perhaps keeping yourself overly busy to avoid doing the things that scare you?

- When you keep doing things that don't work. Doing more of what doesn't work, doesn't make it work. Confess. Give it up. Give new ideas the opportunity to flow in.
- When you're saying "I know. I know. I know," – but you really don't know, try saying, "I don't know. I need help." Or, "I need to learn." There is SO much power in this confession!

How do you know when a confession has worked? From the instant sense of ease and humility you get. When you don't have to pretend anymore, you're free to move forward.

I Get Why You're Exhausted

I was frozen. Panicky. I didn't want to start anything or work on anything. I couldn't focus and my creativity was at zero. I was in pure urgent mode, waiting for the next emergency.

You see, the previous Saturday, my husband (who won't even take an Advil for a headache) walked into my office and said, "I need you to take me to the hospital." Within two minutes he was green, sweating and in the worst pain of his life. It came on out of nowhere, and we had to call an ambulance. It was terrifying.

Prompt medical attention determined that kidney stones were the culprit. Excruciatingly painful, but thankfully not life threatening.

In the weeks following, I found myself in panic mode, flinching every time I heard my husband sigh, I worried that the sudden onset of mind-bending pain and a trip to the emergency room was imminent.

In the midst of this crisis mode, I had a huge revelation.

This is how many people live every day. This is what holds them back. I'm not referring to people in actual emergency situations or even just potentially urgent ones. This is about entrepreneurs, - people like you and me.

We get frozen by this pressing feeling of the urgent and it is **completely false**. I know this firsthand because what is truly important, what is truly urgent, is very, very different from what we **misinterpret as urgent every single day**. But the results are the same: Paralysis, lack of creativity, wanting to shut down, avoid and distract.

We get confused, and it's time to clear up the confusion right now.

Here an exercise to help you distinguish the difference between something that's really urgent and something that just wants to distract you into believing it's urgent.

Situation 1: Imagine you, your child, or your spouse just severely broke their leg. Sink into that feeling. This is truly urgent. Your day needs to be rescheduled. Your email doesn't matter. Your clients need to wait.

Situation 2: Think about your email inbox and the stress you experience over it. This is obviously not urgent, but does it feel different? It should. You can handle this and your life should not be rescheduled because of it.

We cannot treat daily priorities or simple distractions as if they are urgent – at least not for long. We will burn out or give up, because it is just too damned hard to sustain.

Out of Your Mind
(how to get there)

"I'm SO busy."

I'm sure you've either heard this, said this or cried this.

Busy starts in the mind with a feeling of chaos, clutter, and overwhelm. When you're in that kind of head space, everything in your world appears chaotic, cluttered, and overwhelming. You know what this feels like – going a hundred miles an hour in your head, and getting nowhere fast.

Here are seven ways to get out of your mind when the internal busy-ness has you spinning in circles.
1. **Do it.** What are you avoiding? Avoiding projects, whether big or small, can drain your energy more than just taking care of them. For instance, obsessing over your taxes can drain your ability to focus on work, or enjoy your personal life – so just do them and get on with life!
2. **Is this mine?** Ask yourself this question. The busyness in your head may be – at least in part – someone else's problem. Take the time to identify who should actually own the thoughts you're entertaining between your ears – you may find they're not even yours!
3. **Take a hike.** Get out into nature, or simply walk around the block. Especially if you work from home, this is a great way to shake your brain out of a frantic, locked-up pattern.

4. **Write it down.** If you're hashing and rehashing thoughts in your head, writing them down takes away a lot of the fear and worry. It brings them into the realm of reality, and the power they have over you is significantly diminished.

5. **Talk it out.** Sharing what is bothering you gets you out of the spinning in your mind and gets it out in the open. Letting someone else in on the process can give you new, fresh ideas. Be careful, though. If you're talking about the same story over and over, then you're falling into the trap of just complaining, rather than actually looking for solutions.

6. **Laugh.** Go on YouTube and type "funny cats" into the search bar. A little silliness goes a long way in shifting gears in your mind!

7. **Yippee file.** Write down what you've done right today. Include every little thing and acknowledge yourself for what you've done. I created a "Yippee" file where I write down each day's successes.

Overwhelm, Chapter 427

I went to lunch with a good friend who is also a great business woman. She had just returned from a huge business seminar with hundreds of people and tons of information. She said it was like drinking from a fire hose.

She shared with me how overwhelmed she felt, and how she just knew she was missing the boat because there were so many things she hadn't done yet and how everyone else at the event would pass her by.

She's lucky she's got me as a friend, because I very nicely told her to stop being an idiot.

Ok, no, I didn't say that, but I did let her know that everyone gets overwhelmed when bombarded with lots of information all at once. Not to be too cynical, but the very purpose of many of these events is to overwhelm you so you need their next product or service.

But I digress...

The point is, thinking you're the only person who gets overwhelmed is pure self-sabotage.

Everyone gets overwhelmed – even really smart, hardworking, motivated people. When you tell yourself the lie that everyone else has it figured out, and you're just the loser oddball, you are shooting yourself in the foot and stopping your forward momentum.

Now why would we do this to ourselves? Because moving forward means moving into the unknown. It means possibly looking like you're getting too big for your britches and opening yourself up for criticism and rejection. Seriously scary stuff.

Best bet? Create a plan of action and then focus on taking small strategic steps. Engage in opportunities for movement, growth, profit, connection, feeling great, reaching higher, inspiring others, helping more people, and rising above the fray.

When you keep your attention on small steps and the good things ahead, sabotage and overwhelm don't stand a chance.

I Don't Wanna

When I arrived at the hotel on a business trip to Los Angeles, I promptly got sick and spent two days in the hotel room, depressed and feeling lousy. I missed the entire event and headed home.

Once home, I didn't want to do anything. Everything seemed like a huge undertaking and even coffee didn't help.

This is a real problem for entrepreneurs, especially for those of us who work from home in our pajamas a lot of the time. So, what can be done when this heavy inertia settles in?

I came up with a few ideas, as I struggled.

1. **Do ANYTHING.** I wrote this article you are reading as a way to shake free of the doldrums, but it can be as simple as taking a shower, or looking at your to do list and picking the item that looks most appealing (even if it isn't a priority).
2. **Listen to someone else.** Call someone and ask about their life so you can get out of your own head space.
3. **Listen to someone else.** Yes, this is a repeat, but it's a different "someone else." If your inertia is accompanied (as it often is) by a bad attitude, listen to a recording of a motivational speaker or a teacher to get focused on adjusting your mindset.
4. **Go outside.** Nature is a great healer.

5. **Do the task that's been sitting around for a month.** It might be picking up shirts from the dry cleaner, paying library fines, or cleaning out your car. Stagnation in your physical space can lead to stagnation in your mental space.

The Gift in the Exhaustion

I had a cold for a few weeks, and was just miserable. Stuffy head, cough, achy – the usual stuff. Plus my energy was just sapped. Going up one flight of stairs wiped me out.

Unexpectedly, exhaustion provided me with a gift.

In the middle of feeling totally lousy, I was contacted by a friend who told me I needed to create a consulting proposal. No big deal, right? But this was for a project I had been told was mine already, and now I have to basically **apply** for it?

Take my exhaustion and add one part disappointment and one part aggravation.

I still wanted the gig, but at that point I had a terrible cold and an even worse attitude. So I said to myself (very maturely), "FINE. I'll put together your stupid proposal. I'm just going to write whatever comes to mind and that's going to have to be good enough. Screw 'em."

As I put together the proposal, I disengaged that voice in my head that nags me to always be doing better. I honestly just didn't have the energy to both do the proposal and listen to the nag.

What happened was pretty magical. My knowledge flowed out onto the paper and it was excellent. I completed it in less than half an hour, and ended up getting the gig.

Now I strive to keep this gift of disengaging the nagging

voice and let what I know flow out into the world without paralyzing my momentum, worrying that it should be better.

Growing Your Business Only FEELS Like a Shark Attack

In the past, when I heard a business owner talk about expanding their business, the images that came to mind were of sipping piña coladas on a sandy beach, rolling in piles of hundred-dollar bills, and driving a fleet of Mercedes.

<cringe>

Yes, it's embarrassingly naïve. And these pie-in-the-sky images did absolutely nothing to prepare me for the realities of growing a business.

Here are a few things I wish someone had told me about significantly growing a business:

You are going to be scared and excited, feel like you're going to throw up, feel like a champion, feel like a loser; and you're going to feel all of these things, in rotation, on a daily basis - often before lunch. These fears are GROWING pains, but they will feel exactly like the fear and pain of real danger (like there is a shark about to devour you). You must be mentally disciplined enough to step back from your fear and evaluate it. Call it out, and call it what it is…"This is simply a scary-feeling growing pain. This is not a shark attack."

Growth takes longer, and costs more, than you expect. This is just the way it works. So don't beat yourself up, AND budget three times as much time, and twice as much money as you think you're going to need.

You are going to want to give up. Totally normal. When I'm in growth mode, I quit my business at least once a month. Make sure you have a strong support network who can talk you off the ledge when the going (inevitably) gets rough.

You will screw up. When you're growing, you are constantly in uncharted territory and outside your area of expertise. Just be open to turning screw ups into opportunities to discover a new way of doing things. When you keep an open mind, the "wrong" path can lead you to unexpected innovation.

It's ok to work nights and weekends (for a while). When you're getting a new project off the ground, more energy is required. Don't feel guilty for working a lot of hours when you're building something that will free you up significantly in the future! With that being said, also make sure there is a cutoff date for your increased hours.

Isolation is a killer, so get help. You can get so wrapped up in your growth plan that you develop blinders to easy solutions and faster results. Make sure to work with a mentor who can spot the easy solutions you're too overwhelmed to see.

Significantly growing your business is **not** for the faint of heart. Keep going. It's worth it.

Chapter 4

An Entrepreneur Walks into a Dentist's Office

What it Takes to Grow

An Entrepreneur Walks into a Dentist's Office...

I went to the dentist for a regular checkup, and he recommended that I get braces. My first thought was, "Try again pal, I know a sales pitch when I hear one."

Then he went on to show me how my misaligned teeth would over time, damage themselves, wear down, and loosen in their very foundation.

Upon getting a second opinion, the next dentist added, "The good thing is that the correction right now is pretty simple. It won't be too uncomfortable or take long to correct, so it won't be too costly if you correct it now."

I was disappointed because – aside from the unexpected expense – I like my slightly crooked teeth. I think they give me character.

So I had to choose between a fondness for my quirky teeth, or, down the road, possibly losing them all at much pain and expense. Once I had the facts, it was not a tough decision.

Then as I reflected on this experience, I found a strong parallel to entrepreneurship.

Think about it. Is there anything that needs correcting in your business? Maybe it's something that you're fond of, but might be more of a problem than a benefit?

There are often aspects of our business that we like, but that may ultimately be damaging. However, if you discover them early and correct them, they will be less costly, you'll recover more quickly, and the whole process will be less painful.

So how do you consistently make these corrections so you stay in alignment? Simply be consistent about evaluating your business. Review revenue, marketing, goals, team members, and your action plan. Talk to an outside expert. When you do this, you can quickly get back into alignment with your goals. You'll find yourself more focused and energized, as you reach your goals faster than expected.

Get Out of "Too Busy to Grow" Mode

What is it about my brain that, when things are going great, makes it start firing new ideas at me? "Oooohhh... and I could do this, and I could do that, and then I could write a book and start a screenplay and build a better mousetrap..."

You get the idea. And you can probably relate.

If that's the case, here is an easy way out allowing you to calm down, dig deeper and take on only the best opportunities:

1. Write a huge messy list of everything that's on your mind. All the ideas, all the to-do's, all of the fun stuff. Get it out of your head and on paper so it's not making you crazy and distracted.
2. Determine your #1 priority, and write it down.
3. Review your messy list, and identify the items that are most closely related to your #1 priority.
4. Put these items into your calendar. And under-schedule yourself! Believe it or not, you'll get more done, faster if you schedule lightly.

Moral of the story: If you're feeling overwhelmed – either with too much work or too many opportunities – your priority MUST be to take a 'time out' and prioritize.

Raise Your Rates (how & why)

At a speaking engagement, I was interacting with the audience when I was asked, "Why do you constantly talk about raising your rates?"

I replied, "So you can have the freedom to be truly generous with your clients."

The questioner looked confused, so I went on to explain, "You know how sometimes you'll give a client a price break, like a "friends & family" discount, and then you end up resenting the time you take with them? That resentment comes from knowing you could be charging someone else more for that time, or doing something else to grow your business, right? Yeah, I don't recommend you do that."

It's true that you can be generous no matter what you charge, but when you're charging bargain basement prices, can you be *truly* generous? As in, "staying out of resentment and giving from the heart without fear that you're going broke" kind of generous?

Not so much. So how do you resolve the seemingly conflicting ideas of charging more money and being more generous?

Stop confusing offering cheap rates with being generous.

Cheap is solely about money. When you charge cheap rates, you will be inclined to give less. This is where you find yourself thinking thoughts like, "Well, they only paid me this, so I'm only going to give them that. I'll charge them extra if they ask for that." This is a tightfisted, no-fun way to do business. And it's exhausting.

Generous is about value and abundance. When you charge a premium fee for your services, you feel free to give more of yourself.

And what happens for your clients? One, they are more committed to their own success because they are literally more invested. And two, they receive more from you. When you add those two things together, **your clients are more successful and you experience more freedom.**

The usual follow up question I get to this is, "If that's the case, then why don't more business owners raise their rates?"

Well... a million mindset issues plague entrepreneurs when asking for money, like childhood programming, self-worth issues, etc. Instead of going down that road, here's a different approach.

Below is a list of red-flag resentment (RFR) phrases. When you hear yourself thinking or saying them, they will let you know to stop complaining, and instead, recognize you're falling into the trap of trying to be cheap to win business... and it's going to come back to bite you.

RFR: "Don't they know what a great deal I gave them?"
First of all, if you do give someone special pricing, you should definitely let them know. Otherwise, if they're getting a deal and don't know it, you're adding a layer of martyrdom to your resentment. Not a great idea.

Assuming they **do** know they are getting a deal, their excitement over the bargain only lasts through the sales process. Once they hire you, they just expect great service like everyone else.

Tip: While it's fine to have friends and family pricing, make sure those fees are high enough to allow you to be dedicated to your client. To do this, prepare a list of services and pricing with regular and preferred (a.k.a., friends and family discount) pricing. Use this when quoting your rates, and do not give further discounts

RFR: "Don't they know how long it took me to get here and learn all this?"

Ouch. Ok, this is a tough one. Maybe this isn't the exact phrase that runs through your head, so another way to know you're in this bad space is that you feel like you're trying to convince your client of your value at every turn.

Tip: Have a structured sales process with a format that helps prospects understand exactly the problem they need solved, and the value you bring in solving that problem. When you have this structured sales conversation with a prospect, they will feel confident you understand their needs, and it sets the stage for a profitable, successful, respectful client relationship.

RFR: "Don't they know how much time this is taking me?"

This often shows up in business as the hope that your client will suddenly be able to read your mind, recognize how hard you're working for them (probably outside of the scope of your agreement) and offer to pay you more out of the goodness of their heart.

Nope. Never going to happen.

Tip: Create detailed agreements. Agreements should include a clear scope of work, payment agreement, and (maybe most importantly) how work outside the scope of the original agreement will be handled. This is particularly important for creative work like graphic or interior or web design. I highly recommend that in addition to getting a signed agreement, you go through your agreements verbally with your client. "Scope creep" happens all the time in creative work, so making sure there is clear communication around the subject is critical.

Imagine what it would be like to charge rates that are high enough to free you to give generously. All of your work with clients is joyful, and you're not worrying about what else you could be doing to generate income. You establish your value from the beginning so your clients respect and appreciate your work. And you set clear boundaries up front, so they work collaboratively with you to reach their goals.

What would that make possible for you? What stresses would it alleviate?

What does generosity allow *me* to do? I take clients out to dinner. Add free sessions. Send them books. Brainstorm ideas for them outside of our appointment times. Work with their teams. All of these things create stronger relationships, higher levels of commitment and, ultimately, more successes for my clients.

Raise your rates. It's good for the world.

The Question that Keeps You Stuck

I taught a teleclass that focused on tracking activity so business owners could get clear on exactly how to spend their limited time and resources. The key to the process was to reflect on past positive results and uncover the specific actions that led to those repeated successes.

When I asked the participants to share the patterns of success they discovered, I got a variety of responses. Networking, phone calls, social media and more. As I expected, what worked for each business owner was a little different and unique to their skills, preferences, and industries.

Then one participant asked a question. "I can see that networking really worked in the past, but can you give me some ideas for what else I can do?"

Perfect. Do you see what she did there? She identified what worked, but instead of thinking, "WOW, cool, I'm going to do more of what is working," she asked what I hear all the time – the question that keeps you stuck, frantic and overwhelmed: "What else can I do?"

Always asking "what else?" keeps you looking for the next quick fix, distracted by bright shiny objects, and susceptible to slick new marketing schemes. It keeps you from doing the things that will help you reach your goals simply and easily.

What is the smart alternative?

Evaluate your business to discover what actions are producing results and then simply do more of those actions. In a nutshell…

Stop asking, "What else?"

Start asking, "What works?"

Get Your Freedom Back with This One Tip

I was shaking my head because in rapid succession, several clients and colleagues came to me saying, "I was invited to a meeting with [insert name here] and I'm not sure why we're meeting. What should I do?"

I was FLOORED. I know how busy entrepreneurs are. I know how much they value their freedom…how can they afford to take meetings with no clear purpose? And why would they?

In-person meetings take a serious investment of your time, so you must make that investment intentionally. When you invest in the wrong meetings, it wastes hours and hours of your time, creates serious frustration, and keeps you frantic.

The key to investing wisely is to learn how to clarify the purpose and, when appropriate, gracefully say no.

Easier said than done, right? Here are a few tips I use to directly and politely say no to unnecessary meetings:

First, don't automatically say yes to in-person meeting requests! When you receive a request, take a moment to evaluate whether or not there is a clear reason for you to take the time to meet.

Next, clarify the reason for the meeting. Some examples:

- Thanks so much for reaching out to me! So I am clear, what are you hoping to accomplish during our meeting?
- Thanks for suggesting we collaborate. Before we meet, what do you have in mind?
- I appreciate you thinking of me. What do you want to discuss during our meeting?

Believe it or not, many times when I've asked for clarification, the requester simply does not reply and the issue resolves itself.

Say no thank you or suggest an alternative.

If they do reply, and you don't want to take the meeting in-person, here are some diplomatic ways to either say no or suggest a less time-consuming alternative.

- Thanks for clarifying. From what you describe, it sounds like what you're looking to accomplish doesn't really align with what I'm doing. I appreciate you thinking of me, and I'll have to pass now.
- Great, thanks for the details. I'd love to have this conversation with you, and I'd prefer to meet over the phone. Is that something you'd be open to? For a conversation like this, I find the phone saves us both a ton of time.
- I'd love to meet, and I'm not available for an in-person meeting for the next three weeks. Would you mind following up with me then?

The most important thing is to say what you mean.

To keep clear boundaries and intentionally invest your time, do not say you're open to meeting at a later date if you really want to say no. Being unclear will come back to bite you!

Remember this: you are not truly helping anyone when you agree to do things you don't want to do. Saying yes to an obligation that aggravates you prevents the requester from finding someone who would actually be excited about the opportunity. Saying no is sometimes the best gift we can give to others, and to ourselves!

How to Get $1.7 Million
in Business

Let me warn you up front – you are NOT going to like the answer here. I don't even like it. It's too illogical for my Vulcan tendencies.

My husband is a real estate agent, and at one point in his career, he got a $1.7 million listing for a horse ranch. Here's how it happened...

Many years ago, Adam met Jim and Cindy Candle at a networking function. He kept in touch. Three years later, they asked him to sell their property. So Adam took on the listing and sold the property. He kept in touch. The Candles referred him to the Halseys to sell their high-end home. Adam listed their property and kept in touch. The Halseys were so happy with his work, they referred him to the Blartnicks (yes, these are all fictitious names). Adam sold the Blartnicks home and, working his tail off, found them their next home. The Blartnicks were so happy with Adam that they referred him to the Jellywigs (now I'm just having fun). The Jellywigs wanted to sell their home, so Adam went to tour the property. As he was touring, a former client of Adam's came up in conversation as a mutual acquaintance. The Jellywigs knew this client (let's call him Bob), and said they'd tell Bob that they met Adam. Within a week, Adam was contacted by Bob to list his $1.7 million horse property.

Now, in a million years, could Adam have orchestrated this precise sequence of events?

Unlikely. But there are patterns that led to this outcome.

1. He asked people he met if they would give him referrals.
2. He kept in touch.
3. He did a superb job for his clients.
4. He kept in touch.
5. He took the attitude that the universe is plotting to do him good. (aka "reverse paranoia")
6. He kept in touch.
7. He worked consistently and diligently.
8. He kept in touch.

Stay in touch with your clients, it's not the shortest of paths to income, but it's one of the most lucrative!

iPhone/Time Management

Anytime I teach about time management, I imagine the sighs and eye rolls – "Yes, Mary, we're all familiar with time management, thanks so much. Why don't you teach about something exciting, like Social Media or SEO or multiple streams of income?"

What I know for certain is that if you haven't mastered time management, the rest of the stuff isn't going to matter much. I have two stories that illustrate my point.

> **Story #1.** Headed to the beach on vacation in Arroyo Grande, California, I parked the car across from the sand and sea, threw my iPhone in my sweatshirt pocket, and proceeded to jog across the street.
>
> When I heard something crash to the pavement.
>
> Yep, it was my iPhone. It had popped right out of my pocket onto the road, and the glass shattered. I ended up spending the afternoon in an Apple Store instead of at the beach.

This is how we often treat our time. Carelessly. Mindlessly. And we are generally unhappy with the results.

> **Story #2.** One autumn, my hubby and I went to Flagstaff, AZ to ride the ski lift to the top of the mountain, so we could enjoy the golden aspens and the phenomenal view. It was the perfect environment to take some pictures.

I was fifty feet off the ground, and my iPhone didn't have a wrist strap, so I was highly concerned about dropping it, but the view was simply too tempting. So I very deliberately took it out of my purse, took a few photos while handling the phone with extreme care, and then once again deliberately put it back into my purse. I ended up with beautiful photos and a totally intact iPhone.

See the difference? Careless vs. deliberate.

With so many hot opportunities and exciting technologies, it's easy to dismiss the ordinary idea of time management. Managing those tiny moments seems like too great a task, and not worth it.

But the fact is, our lives are **made** out of those tiny moments, often overlooked and carelessly tossed aside.

So what do **your** moments add up to? A careless, haphazard existence, or a fulfilling life created deliberately?

10 Hard Truths About Entrepreneurship

When you become an entrepreneur, you sign up for an amazing journey. A journey that allows for tremendous freedom and limitless financial opportunities.

It also comes with a laundry list of frustrations: long hours, cash flow issues, endless learning curves, hustling for clients, marketing, feast-or-famine income, failures, more marketing, cancellations… and the list goes on.

One reason entrepreneurs stay stuck in these frustrations is simply because of unrealistic expectations. That big gap between what you think entrepreneurial success SHOULD look like and what it ACTUALLY looks like.

Where do these expectations come from? Oh, well, let's see… maybe people selling the idea that we don't need to work hard or have a list of contacts to succeed? Or the constant message that there are magic ways to become an overnight success? Or simply comparing ourselves to people who are succeeding without understanding the years of work that got them there?

We fall into the trap of wanting instant success almost without noticing.

How do you escape the trap?

Accept the hard truths about entrepreneurship.

Here are 10 tips focused on the hard truths of entrepreneurship so you can grow, succeed, and keep your sense of humor throughout the process.

1. **You're going to have to work.** Everyone who has been dubbed an "overnight success" or who has gotten a "big break" that exploded their business put in **years** of work to get there. Any big break comes from consistently knocking on doors, practicing, and never giving up completely.

2. **It's a long term commitment.** Understand from the beginning that building a business is a process, not a one-time event and it takes time. Here's a way to check this: experts consider 20% year-over-year increase a **phenomenal** rate of growth. Successful entrepreneurs will tell you that during their first few years in business, they often felt like a failure. Because they would get one client at a time, not the avalanche of clients they thought they should get. The growth felt agonizingly slow and felt like they were doing things wrong, only to look back years later and realize that the simple consistency in their early years built all of their future successes.

3. **Income must be a central deciding factor.** In a small business, everything competes for attention – marketing, sales, accounting, production, and the list goes on. In all this busyness and noise, decisions made based on the bottom line can get lost in the shuffle and the results are disastrous. When making decisions, you must look at your numbers as a primary guiding influence.

4. **Take time (a lot of time) to work ON your business.** Working IN your business = marketing, seeing prospects and clients, email, meetings, phone calls, accounting. Working ON your business = vision, strategy, planning, evaluation, development. Without working ON your business,

you run the risk of creating a lot of work, but with no direction and poor results.

5. **Get comfortable with being uncomfortable.** Entrepreneurs LIVE outside their comfort zone. Which sounds edgy and cool until you discover it means you always have a degree of "I don't know what the hell I'm doing" going on.

6. **Focus on marketing.** You've heard the saying, "Do what you love and the money will follow." Not true. Or how about, "Build it and they will come." Nope. No matter how brilliant you are or how unique your offering is, you are going to have to actively seek out buyers. No way around it, ever.

7. **Be consistent.** To grow a successful business, it's more effective to take consistent action than it is to engage in sporadic big bursts of activity. Be consistent with your message and you'll become known as the expert in your field. Be consistent with your marketing to get out of the feast-or-famine income cycle. Be consistent with self-care so you can actually enjoy the successes you're building.

8. **Fail, try again, repeat (as quickly as possible).** Even Oprah sucked when she started. But she was willing to suck, then try again and work her way up to being mediocre, and then try over and over and over until she became truly a master at her work. You will fail – it is part of the process, so get used to it. The important thing is to be **willing** to fail, then quickly make adjustments, and try again as quickly as possible so you can achieve mastery as fast as possible.

9. **Invest in mentors.** You will significantly shorten your timeline to success, and lower your stress

levels when you stop trying to figure it all out yourself.

10. Get **used to never being done.** Set goals, yes, and achieve them. But entrepreneurs are hard-wired to always look for the next opportunity. As you're achieving one goal, you're already seeing the next one – or the next ten!

Bottom line? Entrepreneurship is not for the faint of heart, nor for the "get-rich-quick" seeker.

It's for hearty souls like you. It's for workers. It's for believers and impact-makers. Champions who are tough enough to persevere when obstacles arise, and humble enough to ask for help to ensure their success.

Chapter 5

Imaginary Obstacles

Your Brain, Your Mindset

Imaginary Obstacles

I was working with a client to create an action plan to help him reach his goals quickly. We boiled it all down to simple steps, and right away he saw how the whole thing would work. In his words, he was inspired with a plan.

He was so confident, in fact, his next words were, "I'm not sure I can handle all the business this will create. I'd better cut back on the actions a little so I'm not overwhelmed."

WOW. What happened?

Self-sabotage, that's what.

When faced with a plan to quadruple his income, he found that he was WAY outside his comfort zone.

His self saboteur immediately threw obstacles in his path. **Imaginary obstacles.**

Imagined problems. Imagined stresses. Imagined failures.

Undetected, these imaginary obstacles could have prevented him from taking action, and just invisibly sabotaged his efforts.

Don't shrink back in the face of imagined problems that might accompany success. Create your plan in alignment with your goals and values. Be consistent about implementing your plan. Track your results. And tackle obstacles **only** when they actually show up.

A Sneaky Little Sucker

Success rarely looks like you expect.

I can give you a great example of a time when I had just successfully launched a huge new training program and then almost shut down completely.

After weeks of preparation for the launch webinar, writing a sales page, working with a sales coach, a business coach and a web designer, preparing course content, and administrative systems galore... here is what the day of the webinar looked like:

1. I gave the webinar while sitting on my couch, very prepared, but nervous as hell.
2. Results: great attendance, great feedback, great enrollments for my program.
3. EUPHORIA!!! People enrolled! I'm profitable!!!!!
4. I'm REALLY tired (I was so excited I didn't sleep the night before!)
5. Now I have to put the finishing touches on the materials. I'm even more tired.
6. Why didn't more people enroll?
7. I still need to promote this to have a few more people enroll.
8. I'm exhausted... what was I thinking?

I went from nervous to euphoric to exhausted self-doubt in a matter of an hour. You know what I call this?

NORMAL.

Whenever you make a BIG stretch outside your comfort zone, your comfort zone wants to snap back to its original dimensions. And it's a sneaky little sucker. It will use all the tricks in the book to get you to believe that this discomfort is harmful as opposed to what it really is: **growth**.

Here are a few examples of the kinds of thoughts that creep in to hold you back; compliments of your comfort zone:

1. Exaggeration: "I'm tired now. What if I'm tired ALL the time? I'd better stop this."
2. Diminishment: "You only had 16 people sign up? You should have had 50. It wasn't worth it."
3. Judgment: "You're a fraud. Everyone is going to find out that you don't know what you're talking about."
4. Pure self- doubt: "Who do you think you are?

After that launch, I spent a rough few days with these kinds of thoughts about myself. And when you get into this icky headspace, I recommend you do what I did.

Talk to colleagues and friends, eat chocolate, work out, and watch mindless television. Do whatever you need to do to endure the discomfort of growth in order to expand your comfort zone.

How to Get Committed

I was fretting over a big project that would keep me on the road a lot, plus the demands of seeing my regular clients, writing blogs, creating a new program, etc. I started to get paralyzed by it all, when a thought popped into my head...

"How committed am I to feeling this way?"

Hmm...I hadn't thought of it that way before. Strangely, the question made me smile. Who intentionally commits to something like a lousy attitude? The heavy stress that was starting to take over was instantly lifted, although I'm not exactly sure why.

Maybe a little humor simply helped me refocus on what I wanted to accomplish, rather than dwelling on the obstacles.

Maybe the question reminded me of the things I AM committed to – loving my family, serving others, enjoying life. Powerful things that, when compared with how I was feeling, made the idea of committing to a bad attitude seem ludicrous.

Maybe it's because I moved from the "I am stress" perspective, to the "I have stress." Things that you ARE, can't be easily removed. Things that you HAVE, can be gotten rid of with a simple decision.

Whatever the reason, the shift was significant and immediate. It was like getting a deep breath of fresh air after being in a stuffy, smoke-filled room. Aaahhh... that's better!

Tea and Reality

A few years back, I decided to make a pot of fragrant herbal tea. I set a big pot on the stove, added the tea, set the timer for 22 minutes, and went into another room to read. When the timer went off, I looked up from my book, and immediately smelled the sweet tea.

What struck me as interesting is that I didn't smell the tea until **after** the timer beeped. Strange. Think of it – was the tea fragrance in the air before timer went off? Of course it was. But because my attention was elsewhere, I didn't notice it. In my world, it didn't exist.

It occurred to me that this was a perfect example of how our focus impacts our perception of reality.

There are opportunities right under our nose every day, but because of a simple lack of focus, they can go completely unnoticed.

So work on your mindset. This does not mean being happy-happy all the time. It means developing the discipline to direct your thinking. Without mental discipline, your thinking will follow old patterns, and you'll overlook opportunities that are right in front of you.

Banging Your Head Against the Wall

We all know the analogy of banging your head against the wall, and how good it feels when you stop, right? In that same vein, over the past several years, I noticed that right before I experience a great big a-ha moment, I had days, weeks, or even months of head-banging frustration. Wanting to get things to move and change right now right now right now!

Not that I'm impatient or anything.

Oh, and did I mention that I never remember this pattern in the midst of the frustration but only in hindsight?

One time on an ordinary day, I was in the shower and started feeling that familiar stress, and I immediately wanted all my worries to be sorted and solved right now right now right now. As usual, my mind started doing laps around the things I was worried about, but then something new and different happened.

I said to myself, "Wait! I remember this feeling. I don't have to freak out, this just means change is coming. And if I recall correctly, things always work out in perfect time. I can relax." Weird, right? But it gets weirder.

I took a deep breath, and WHOOSH! A great solution to my problems flooded into my mind. I was so stunned that I actually had to put out a hand and steady myself against the tile.

It seems that by letting go of the need to solve everything right away, space was created that allowed solutions to flow in.

Leveraging Old Tapes

While in my favorite thinking place (the shower), I was getting more and more stressed out. Thoughts raced through my head, "There's not enough time. I don't do enough marketing. I don't have enough events…"

Understand that the "not enough" theme is the most damaging old tape that runs through my head. In good times, I'm conscious of it and can manage it, but in times of stress, it induces panic.

But then something great happened. My crazy self-talk was halted by an unexpected voice of reason.

It said, "Wait a minute. Not enough? Ok… in other words, I'd like more. So how do I get more? Be grateful for what I have, be open to receive more, and get to work on the things that are in alignment with these thoughts."

A much nicer way to express "not enough", don't you think?

Recognize!

After proudly announcing that I had just gone national with my networking event, my husband said to me, "No you didn't."

Huh?

He said, "You went national LAST year when you did your event in Michigan."

Forehead slap! How could I have forgotten that?

The answer is simple – I'm an entrepreneur. I'm always looking at what is next. How can I grow? How can I go further? Innovate? Help more people?

And in the process, I forget to acknowledge what I've accomplished. Forget completely.

High-achievers are probably shrugging their shoulders right now and saying to themselves, "Yeah? So what? You can't rest on your laurels and recount yesterday's tales of glory."

To them I say, well, yes... and no.

An internationally renowned psychologist emphasizes the importance of acknowledging our accomplishments.

Broadly paraphrasing here, she says that if you are focused on making changes in your life you MUST continuously acknowledge your accomplishments. The makeup of your brain needs this positive reinforcement in order to change the physical connections that contribute to lasting change. Lack of acknowledgement gives your brain the message, "Yeah, I know I did some good things today, but they aren't that great (and not important enough to retain)."

So your brain can stay stuck in the same patterns, with the same connections, and the same outcomes.

So today – recognize yourself. Your brain (and your goals,) will thank you!

How to Make Everything Easier (seriously!)

Any time you encounter confusion, stress, or indecision, I have a tip that can help every single time. Seriously.

Simply ask yourself, "Am I open to the possibility for this to be easy?"

Some examples:

- Stressed out about a deadline? Ask yourself, "Am I open to the possibility that it could be easy to meet my deadline?"
- Struggling with a problem? Ask yourself, "Am I open to the possibility that I can discover an easy solution?"
- Worried about a conflict? Ask yourself, "Am I open to the possibility that there is an easy resolution?"

When you shift your focus away from the problems and the chaos, your stress level goes down and simpler solutions become apparent.

Blinded by Focus

A couple months ago, I ran into a grocery store to quickly pick up a bottle of water. I was in a hurry, so I sped around, scanning the items on the signs over each aisle for water. No dice. Frustrated, I did another lap around the store and still, no water.

Exasperated, I finally slowed down and found a directory. It indicated that the water was on aisle 10. I headed over, looked up at the items on the aisle 10 sign, and STILL didn't see water listed on the sign. At that point, I started thinking I was crazy, so I looked again, and there it was: "Bottled Water".

I walked by exactly what I wanted time and time again, because I was so focused on what I thought SHOULD be there, that I literally became blind to what was actually there.

A parallel can be struck with goals: be clear about what you want, but keep an open mind in case it shows up in a different form than you expect.

Turn it on its Head

When driving to Sedona one day, I realized that 10 miles had gone unnoticed. I was in my head, coming up with ideas and solutions, and imagining sharing these ideas with friends and clients.

Needless to say, I was not "in the moment".

I started in on the lovely self-talk, "What's wrong with you? You really have to work on getting present. Experience the moment. Maybe I should meditate. I'll talk to Sarah about meditating. But what if she's busy? I've been meaning to tell her about this class I took… "

Whoops! I slid off into mental la-la land again and then started judging myself again.

But then I stopped because suddenly it struck me how natural my internal dialog felt. The wanderings and wonderings just felt like ME. Perhaps this mental flow was not a fault, but rather a gift.

How we manage our so-called "faults" is incredibly important. Some people work to improve them, while others ignore them. I encourage the third option that I stumbled upon the other day – leverage them. Let me give you an example…

I am inherently lazy. It's true. I never want to spend more time on a project than absolutely necessary. How did I leverage laziness?

I translated my laziness (working as little as possible) into efficiency (working smarter, not harder). Same motivation, but when laziness is turned on its head from a fault to a gift, it works for me, rather than against me. I leveraged my natural tendency towards sloth to serve me better.

But back to my "fault" of not being present. How could I possibly leverage the "gift" of drifting off in my mind, thinking about how I'll tell others what I'm experiencing?

Then it hit me – I already learned how to leverage it... I am a storyteller.

Ambition Can Make
You Feel Like a Loser
(even when you're winning)

I was moping around because I wasn't making a million dollars a day, or some other such "realistic" expectation. I moved on to kicking myself for all the things I hadn't accomplished yet, and all of the things I haven't perfected.

Isn't it frustrating how being an ambitious big thinker can make you feel like you're a loser?

This is a common hazard for entrepreneurs. We always see that next goal, that next accomplishment, so even as we are achieving our goals we're simultaneously aware of how we are falling short.

Then a memory popped into my mind that helped put things into perspective.

Several years ago I made my first significantly-priced offer to an audience. I was completely terrified, and ended up with a brutal migraine that lasted three days. I was close to swearing off speaking engagements entirely after that experience, thinking I just wasn't cut out for it.

That memory made me reflect on how far I'd come. These days, I make that same "significantly-priced offer" without batting an eye, make really good money, and migraines are not part of the process.

So if you're feeling frustrated looking up at a seemingly unreachable peak at the top of the mountain, this is my suggestion: take stock of how far you've come. There are things you're doing today that in the past would have terrified you. Instead of kicking yourself for what is left to do, look at what you've overcome, what you've learned, and appreciate even the small steps you've made.

Use this appreciation as validation of your abilities, and the fuel in your tank to rocket you to that next big goal.

Chapter 6

Ditch the Deposits and Go to Vegas

The Day-to-Day

Ditch the Deposits and Go to Vegas

When my husband Adam and I were in the early stages of planning our wedding, we observed several couples who were stressed out and complaining about planning their weddings. I was puzzled. I mean, you get to taste cake, play with flowers, and try on pretty dresses. What's not to love?

In a rare case of foresight, we consciously decided to have fun during the eight months of planning our wedding. If it stopped being fun, we either needed to adjust our attitudes, or ditch the deposits and go to Las Vegas for a quickie wedding.

So we focused on making it fun. We kept an eye on our attitudes. We didn't let other people's opinions sway us from our vision of our perfect day. We (or at least I) really didn't want to get married by Elvis in the Hunka Hunka Burnin' Love Chapel.

Guess what? It was a blast. All eight months of it.

But think of it – 240 days of planning for one day of fun. 99.583% of that time we were on the journey to the wedding, rather than at the destination. If we had let ourselves get totally stressed out for that 99.583% of time, we might never have even made it to the wedding!

So my question to you is – do you treat your business this way?

Do you consciously decide to enjoy it on a daily basis, consider your opinions and priorities first, and create a plan of attack that is fun?

Too often, this is not the case. We struggle to do things the way someone else says we should, allowing ourselves to believe that if we suffer today, we'll see a payoff later.

You know what the business owner's version of the Elvis Chapel is... getting a job! Don't do it!

Great Greetings, Batman!

Believe it or not, you can make a huge shift in your business by simply changing your voicemail greeting. Think about it – your outgoing voicemail greeting makes a first impression on prospective clients. What does yours say about you?

Here is a typical voicemail greeting:

"Hi, thanks for calling the Bat Cave. We're either fighting crime or away from our desks right now, but your call is very important to us, so please leave a message and we'll get back to you as soon as possible."

Although there is nothing inherently wrong with this greeting, it is just vague, and makes a neutral impression on callers. Now let's break it down from the perspective of a caller:

"Hi, thanks for calling the Bat Cave." (oh good, I've got the right number)

"We're either fighting crime or away from our desks right now," (all I know is you're not answering your phone, and I don't really care what you're doing.)

"but your call is very important to us," (hmm...is it really?)

"so please leave a message and we'll get back to you as soon as possible." (what time is, "as soon as possible" exactly? I need to know when I can expect a response.)

Callers really aren't interested in what you're doing if you're not answering your phone. They want a pleasant voice, a brief greeting and most of all, they want to know when you will get back to them. Here are a few tips to keep in mind when creating a professional voicemail greeting:

1. Give your name and company name.
2. Ask for information you need to move the communication along. For example, "I'm available for appointments on Tuesday and Thursday between 1 and 4pm. Leave two dates and times that will work for you and I'll call back to confirm."
3. Avoid making your voicemail an extensive commercial for your business. Example: "Whether you need help with your evil arch enemy, bank robbers, nasty villains, or pesky bad guys in general, Batman and Robin can help. Due to our rapid transportation options, we gladly accept clients from all over North America. With a strong grasp on technology and a commitment to being your partner in all aspects of crime fighting, Batman and Robin can be a key component in keeping your city streets safe..." You get the picture.
4. Let callers know **when** they can expect a response. And by the way, it doesn't matter if you commit to respond by phone within 24 hours, or with an email within 72 hours. Just let callers know what to expect, and then follow through.
5. Let callers know **how** they will get a response from you (email, text, phone)

Here is an example of a good voicemail greeting:

"Hi, you've reached Batman. My office hours are Monday through Friday, 9am to 4pm. Please leave a message and I'll return your call within one business day. For more immediate assistance, or for answers to brief questions, send a text to the same number you just dialed. Thanks for calling."

When callers hear this greeting, they get the impression of an organized and professional business, and that their time is valued and respected.

I recently worked with a seamstress to streamline her business practices. At my suggestion, she changed her voicemail greeting. The immediate feedback from her clients was that they felt more confident about her business after hearing her voicemail greeting. She improved her credibility by simply refining her voicemail greeting!

The Busy Barrier

One of my HUGE pet peeves is when people run around like crazy, saying "I'm so busy, I'm so busy!"

I'm not sure precisely why it bugs me, but I think it has something to do with the underlying message that you are basically a victim to time.

I came embarrassingly face-to-face with this the other day when a friend called and she started the conversation with, "I won't take up much of your time, I know you're so busy."

I told her that I LOVED that she called, and why would she think she couldn't take my time? And then it hit me…

I had constructed a "busy barrier". Without doing so consciously, I'd been repeating "I'm so busy" as a mantra. As a result, I've created a wall that kept people away in both my personal and professional lives. Ouch.

As I wondered how this might negatively impact my business I immediately thought of an example that made me cringe.

There is a business owner I know who is always late to meetings, out of breath, and talking about how insanely busy she is. Recently I had some business that I could have sent her way, but I didn't want to use her. Why?

1. It didn't seem like she had the time for more business.
2. I didn't feel confident in her attention to detail.
3. I worried that she won't get the work done on time.

Then came the really painful part... looking in the mirror and realizing that I'm probably creating the same kind of reactions in people I meet.

So I'm using myself as a cautionary tale for your benefit. By all means, be busy, but be careful what you're communicating to the people around you!

Want to Network Better?
Listen in Neutral

I was talking with my father on a recent trip to visit my parents, and he was reflecting on some lessons he learned in the workplace before he retired. He mentioned that at one point in his career, he attended a team building workshop, and experienced immediate success by implementing some of the teachings.

I asked him what was the best thing he learned, and he replied, "Listening in neutral."

Ah. Good one. Listening in neutral means really hearing what someone is saying, without using it as simply a basis to formulate your own response.

Dad didn't realize that he had just provided me with exactly the answer I'd been looking for with regards to networking.

You see, I teach business people to network with a goal, but without an agenda. For the longest time, I had a hard time explaining the difference. "Listening in neutral" is a big part of the answer.

The goal of networking is always to connect. Listening in neutral is the first step in connecting. Here are some thoughts on the benefits of listening, and the danger of not listening:

- In our busy world of interruptions, the simple act of being present and fully listening is a gift. Any time you give someone a gift, the recipient will want to return the favor.

- You can listen for their needs, rather than just pushing your agenda. When you're pushing your agenda, you're generally pushing people away.
- When you don't listen to someone fully, they know it! Not only that, when someone feels they aren't being heard, toxins are released in their body. Then they start to associate you with feeling toxic – not a great impression!

With all of this in mind, why on earth wouldn't we listen fully?

For myself, I used to worry that I'd get so absorbed in listening that I'd forget to introduce my own business to the conversation. What I found is that when I really listen, and am genuinely curious about others, they always become curious about me.

One Time Management Tip

Create and prioritize your to-do list the night before.

That's the tip.

Doesn't seem like a big deal, does it? Why is it so important?

1. Overnight, your mind works out creative solutions to your tasks while you sleep.
2. From the moment you wake up, you are calmer and clearer, with a sense of purpose for your day.
3. The majority of people are most focused before noon. Rather than wasting this peak mental time on building your task list, you spend it completing those top priority items.

That's it! This one change in your routine reduces stress, increases efficiency and improves your attitude on a daily basis.

Make Sure Your Emails Get Attention

Recently I received a series of emails from a committee I'm on that are absolutely confounding. They were packed with details and usually included several attachments. They were written with multiple fonts, plus bold and italics being used with no rhyme or reason to the emphasis. It took me forever to get through the emails, and, in the end, I was still unclear about whether or not I needed to do anything!

The good news? I was inspired to write this article. You're welcome!

Whether your emails include a sales offer, or simply a question you need answered promptly, here are my top seven tips to get your emails more attention!

1. **Move your reader right away with your subject line.** If you need a response, ask for one right in your subject line, i.e. "NEED RESPONSE ASAP". I definitely capitalize when it's urgent. My most effective subject line ever is "Quick question."

2. **Keep it short.** Especially if you use the subject line "Quick question", don't write a novel, or include an entire sales page. When I'm doing speaking inquiries (and this has worked for people looking for funding and corporate training opportunities as well), I use the "Quick question" subject line, and simply write, "Hi! Could you let me know the process for being considered as a speaker for your group?" I get a response about 90% of the time from complete strangers.

3. **Keep the fonts consistent.** If you use a variety of fonts, your reader's brain gets distracted trying to absorb both the message and the inconsistent fonts. This draws attention away from your message and call to action.

4. **If you have more than one point, number or bullet-point the list.** Visually, this makes it clear what your reader should be paying attention to. Ideas can get lost in the middle of paragraphs and you can lose your reader's attention.

5. **End with ONE question.** If you want to start a conversation to build rapport, end with a question. My speaking inquiry above is an example of this and here's one more; "I'd like to be able to refer you, so could you describe your ideal client to me?"

6. **If there's something you need your reader to do, make sure it is crystal clear.** If you have a call to action – even if it is just a request to respond – make sure it is visually separate from the rest of the content.

7. **If you really want a response from someone, email them individually.** When people know they're in a crowd of others receiving an email, they think they can hide and don't need to respond.

Reality Check About Simplifying

A lot of people are focusing on simplifying their lives. And even though simplifying can eventually rocket you into a Zen-like state, the process can make you want to tear your hair out!

I'll give you an example. Have you ever organized a messy closet? Here's what it looks like:

1. You can't take the chaos anymore, and decide you're going to organize the closet.
2. You pull everything out. It now looks worse (WAY worse) than when you started.
3. You start thinking that it didn't really look that bad to start with, and wonder what possessed you to take on this stupid project in the first place.
4. You go to Starbucks to refuel.
5. You come back and start madly sorting into piles.
6. You start to see some order in the chaos.
7. Tired and sweaty, you put everything away.
8. You sigh with satisfaction, then post the before and after photos on Facebook to make your friends jealous.

The important thing to notice is that **6 out of 8 steps are messy, frustrating, and have you questioning your sanity.** They are exactly the times when you will feel like giving up. But if you give up in the middle of the process, you're going to be in far worse shape than when you started.

If your business, life, or closet is messy right now, keep going or it's going to just get worse. Here are some tips to help you persevere through the chaos:

1. When simplifying anything, don't expect to go from zero to Zen in an hour.
2. If it's messy, know that you're not doing things wrong, you're just in middle of the simplification process.
3. When you feel like giving up, rest and refuel. Eat, nap, call a friend or coach.
4. Know that giving up will create greater chaos than you started with.
5. Keep your eyes on your goal.
6. Acknowledge your successes, and reward yourself.

Cornered!

Scenario #1: You're at a business networking event, and are approached by an enthusiastic woman. She says to you, "You really need to try my vitamins. You'll feel healthy, more energetic, and get more done every day. When would you like to set up an appointment to meet?"

Scenario #2: You're at a business networking event, and are approached by an enthusiastic man. He says to you, "You know a lot of people, right? Here are 5 of my business cards for you to give out to people you know."

Scenario #3: You're at a business networking event, and are approached by a man. He says to you, "Have you ever heard of my company? It's been around for 24 years and was founded in a small town in Northern California where the trees are tall and the land is wild. It's in this wilderness that a new vision was born, a vision of prosperity, a vision of hope, a vision of endless possibilities. Our founder was born in 1965 in a small town in Massachusetts. How did he get from Massachusetts to California? I'll tell you the whole story…"

If you've ever been to a networking event, it's likely you've felt cornered by at least one of these situations. So how do you deal with them?

You can just let these well-meaning folks monopolize your time, leaving you feeling resentful for the time you wasted.

Or you can cut them off and walk away. Not a terrible solution, but it still defeats the purpose of networking, which is to create connections.

Instead, try the following responses the next time you're cornered.

Scenario #1 Response: "I don't need your product now, but if you can be specific about the kind of client you're looking for, I'll definitely keep my eye out for them. Give me one of your cards so that I'll have your information when I cross paths with good referrals."

Scenario #2 Response: "I love referring the people I know to the services they need, but would need to know more about who your ideal client is. If you can be specific about the kind of client you're looking for, I'll definitely keep my eye out for them. I'll keep one of your cards so I can send them your way."

Scenario #3 Response: (interrupting them) "Let me stop you for a second, if you don't mind. I do want to know more about what you do, and what would be most helpful to know is specifics about the kind of client you're looking for, so that I can keep my eye out for them. Give me one of your cards so that I'll have your information when I cross paths with good referrals."

You'll notice a common thread through them all, of course. Each of these responses positions you as the expert networker, someone who is interested in connections and service, even when approached in a less than professional manner. They allow you to create relationships instead of resentments.

Solve Sales Call
Reluctance in 1 Step

"How do I **make** myself do phone calls?"

I have heard this question again and again from clients in industries ranging from financial planning to direct sales to graphic design. There are even coaches who have built their entire practices teaching strategies to get on the phone without fear. **But the truth is, there are only a small handful of business owners who absolutely must get on the phone in order to succeed.**

I have a different approach, and I know you'll like it. Are you ready for the one step to solve your call reluctance? Here it is:

Step 1: Stop wasting your time making phone calls, and instead invest your energy in activities that you'll do with confidence and without resistance.

Why is this so important?

Resistance wastes valuable time. Even if phone calling has brought results in the past, if you take 4 days to work up the nerve to pick up the phone, you've wasted 4 days you could have been emailing or texting or in some other way reaching out to potential clients.

Times have changed. Stop buying the myth that phone calls are the end-all be-all of marketing activities. Phone calls used to be accepted as most effective way to reach people. These days, the majority of people don't answer their phones, many don't listen to voicemail, and most tend to want to spend as little time on the phone as possible. Phone calling is no longer the gold standard for communication with prospects.

No, it's not a cop-out. Don't judge yourself for deciding not to make phone calls, and to move on to actions you don't resist and actually (gasp!) enjoy. It's your business. You're allowed to make executive decisions on how to run it. You have tons of options: email, social media, note cards, texting. Find alternative activities that work for your prospects, and lead to the results you want.

So give yourself a break. Keep consistently reaching out to prospects, just do it in a way that doesn't stress you out.

Distractions and Solutions

In a recent poll, I asked for business owners to share the biggest distractions they face each day. I'm including the top three here, with a few tips to overcome them.

WARNING #1: All of these tips will require you to change. Distractions are a part of life, and trying to eliminate them is impossible – you've got to manage yourself.

WARNING #2: These tips are basics, and you are likely to think, "Well I already know that!" You may know it, but are you DOING it? Don't let the "I know" syndrome lead you away from a deceptively simple tip that could be the solution you need!

#3 Top Distraction: Email

I was surprised this wasn't #1, actually! So how do you deal with the incessant email onslaught that pulls you away from your priorities?

- Turn off all notifications. This means all sounds, visual alerts, icon pop-ups – everything.
- Turn off automatic send and receive. This means you receive email when YOU decide.
- Add checking your email to your schedule like an appointment. I check at 10:30am and 3pm.
- No one sends me emergency emails, so even a response time of 24 hours is appropriate in my business.

Basically, you must reframe how you think about email. It is a communication tool, NOT a priority manager.

#2 Top Distraction: Daily Operations

And I'll lump in another category, "busy work". The best thing to do to deal with the pull of daily operations is to have superior priority and time management habits. I teach an entire class on this, but will keep it simple here with just a few tips.

- Plan your day the night before. If you start working before planning your day, you may not get it planned until noon. And then, seriously, what's the point? But when you go into your office clear about your priorities, and then others make demands of your time, you'll easily be able to discern where new demands fit into your plan.
- Close the door. If you're in an office, this is a literal suggestion. If you work from home, then it means turning off the phones, internet and email so that you can work on that priority list. With focus, you will complete your list in much less time than you expect, and manage the rest of your day (and the people in it) much more cheerfully!

#1 Top Distraction: The Internet

With pop-up notifications, social media, chat, and icons showing us how many "friends" we have waiting, is it any surprise we are distracted by the internet? The internet is a distraction machine, and because it won't change, **you** must change.

- Don't leave social media running while you're working on projects that require concentration.

- Change your web browser home page from one with flashy articles that will distract you to something simple like Google.

The bottom line: Manage your environment so nothing cuts in line in front of your priorities!

Lesson from a TV Funeral

I recently gained a new perspective when, of all things, I was watching a TV show.

I saw a program where they showed a military funeral, and I was awed by the absolute precision and care they took to fold the flag. It struck me as a demonstration of profound courtesy, honor and respect.

It made me wonder, "Do I take care to convey the respect I have for my family, friends, and clients?" And I reluctantly admitted that the answer was, "Usually."

Until seeing this fictional funeral, I hadn't associated attention to detail as a way of conveying my respect for others. I came up with recommendations to outwardly show courtesy, honor and respect:

- Show up on time for meetings and appointments
- Respond to email & phone calls in a timely manner
- Pay attention to details with written communications
- Dress with care
- Promptly thank others when they are helpful

All of the above can also be seen as strategies to demonstrate professionalism, which is how I've viewed them for a long time. From my new perspective of taking care to honor others, these actions take on an even more powerful role.

Time Management FAIL

One Monday, I had a short list of easily accomplishable tasks, and a small amount of time to do them. I was going through my list one item at a time, and then my first appointment of the day cancelled.

I thought – oh cool. Now I'm going to get that calendar scheduling program set up, update all my social media profiles, and start organizing our move to California.

FAIL!

Why is it when time opens up, we cram it with twice as much stuff? Notice I didn't even consider doing something relaxing like taking a walk or going to a yoga class!

Nope. Here's what I did:

1. I immediately stopped looking at my original list, so my priorities got lost in the shuffle.
2. I took that unexpected space in my calendar and tried stuffing it full of other items.
3. By filling the open space, I choked out room for new things to come in. It's basically like saying, "No thanks, universe, don't give me anything else. My time is CHOCK full. And if it isn't, I'll just make myself busy. Don't bother me with new clients or opportunities."
4. When I became aware of what I was doing, I quickly outlined this article, then went back to my priorities. (good job, Mary!)

The lessons here are twofold:

First, when space opens up in your schedule, finish your original priorities, and then consider taking the rest of the day off. Enjoy some of the freedom that is supposed to be a part of the entrepreneurial experience.

And second, build some open space into your schedule. If you literally don't have a second to spare in your day, where is the room to grow?

Lost in the Shuffle: The Bottom Line

I've spoken with a lot of people, and I hear the same frantic questions and concerns...

"What is my marketing plan? Who is my ideal client? I think I need to do search engine optimization. I have to incorporate social media. Should I brand myself? How do I control my email? I need to network more often. How do I generate more referrals?"

In all of this spinning and worrying, do you notice one factor that **is not** mentioned? **Money.**

Business owners can get so tangled up in strategy that they make the mistake of overlooking whether or not money is flowing into the businesses. Trust me on this, I know what I'm talking about. At one point in my entrepreneurial career, I got so caught up in finding the perfect strategies, branding, and systems for my business that I forgot how to stay in business.

Confession time: I got so caught up in the chaos I went bankrupt. Literally.

I don't share this story often, because it is painful and embarrassing. No one likes to admit they totally screwed up in the money department. But it's so important to understand how taking your eye off your income can lead to being out of business, out of your home (yes, I lost my house, too), and totally demoralized.

Why do business owners take their eyes off money?

1. They don't want to be seen as greedy.
2. They are so focused on serving others that they forget to take care of their own needs.
3. They think if they build it, clients will come.
4. They are afraid of the reality of their situation.
5. They confuse busyness, recognition, and involvement for profitability.

So what can you do to combat this confusion and lack? Look your cash flow squarely in the eye and...

- Let go of what isn't working
- Look for additional income streams
- Keep track of the money coming in
- Tie your goals, strategies and actions to income

Chapter 7

Stop Settling for Small Successes

Growing Bolder

Stop Settling for Small Successes

You know what I've noticed?

People settle for small successes all the time. It is disheartening, because they leave so much opportunity, so much positive impact, and so much money on the table.

Why on earth would anyone settle? Well it makes sense when you consider...

1. There is an emotionally happy charge that comes from any success – even small ones.
2. You already know how to accomplish the small successes.
3. Small successes don't make your stomach drop and your palms sweat.

Bottom line: small successes are easy and comfortable.

So how do you move past the settling phase?

1. Recognize when you're settling.
2. Be willing to be uncomfortable in the short term in order to create bigger successes in the long term.
3. Decide on a big opportunity you want to go after.
4. Create the action plan to get there.
5. Implement it, even if it makes your palms sweat.

Stop settling for small successes. You are capable and strong, and deserve great things!

Stick with It, or Change?

My husband and I were working in a coffee shop in Oceanside, CA one day, right across the street from the ocean. He took a break, walked down to the end of the pier and back, and then related this story to me.

"I saw 30+ fishermen on the pier and at least 50 lines in the water. No one was catching fish. And there were no fish in the buckets – I checked. All those fishermen, but no fish."

Weird, right? I mean, if their goal was to catch fish, it was quickly obvious that this was NOT the right place to do it. So why do they all keep coming to the same place doing the same things?

Probably because their thought processes go something like this:

- Everyone is fishing here, so there must be fish here.
- If I'm not catching fish, I should just be patient a little longer before considering changing.
- And I've always fished here anyway... so results be damned – I'm staying!

Crazy, right? But it's SO easy to get caught up in these assumptions and inertia, whether you're fishing or running a business. The trick is to know when to stick with it and be patient, and when to move on and change your strategy.

Stick with it when you are confident that your course of action has a proven record of bringing you the results you want, and nothing has significantly changed in your industry. Sometimes

144

the solution is to just stay the course with consistent, effective actions.

Change your strategy when you are not getting any results in any 60-90 day period, or when something significant has changed in your business, such as your goals, target market, industry, or product offerings.

Assumptions and inertia are often deeply ingrained and can be hard to recognize when left to our own devices. If you change your course of action when you should stick, you'll constantly be in frantic reinvention mode. Stick when you should change, and you'll stay stagnant and frustrated. Either way, your income and sanity suffer.

So get an outside perspective from an expert. Talk to a mentor, consult with a trusted advisor or hire a coach to sort through your options and move forward quickly.

Maybe it's Time to Open the Door

I did something unusual a few years back... I opened the door. My front door, that is, to a couple of clean-cut Mormon boys.

Ok, don't hate me, but when I spy these kind souls through my peephole, I usually quietly watch from behind the door, hoping they'll simply think no one is home and move along to the next house.

But on this particular day it occurred to me that I knew how to handle this situation with ease and grace, and perhaps a little more dignity than I have in the past. So I took a deep breath, and I opened the door.

I was able to look these young men in the eye, thank them for their good works, and gently disagree. We shared a laugh about an old friend of mine who spent her Mormon mission going to seedy bars in Salt Lake City because, as she put it, "Don't you think those people need it the most?" Then I wished them well as they moved along to the next house.

Why did I find this situation significant? Because I realized it was good practice for real life.

I'm sure I'm not the only person who finds it stressful to be in situations where I disagree or I have to say no. But what I know for sure is that when I don't deal with these situations, the stress internalizes itself. Over time, it builds, it erupts, and it can even cause health problems.

So, is there anything that you are "hiding behind the door" from? Would it be possible to kindly look it in the eye and let it move out of your life?

Maybe it's time for you to open the door, too.

One Way to Have More Fun

I love teaching business processes – a potentially deadly dull subject – and have an audience light up with understanding and relief that their business can be so much easier!

As I reviewed a video of a recent presentation, I started thinking, "Uh-oh, I don't look like other professional speakers."

I noticed that I laughed a bit too much, my hand gestures weren't crisp, I strayed from my outline, and overall, I just looked, well… different. Cataloging the things I needed to change left me feeling a bit flat.

Then I reviewed the experience again in my mind. The audience was engaged and participating. They laughed with me. They gave me immediate feedback about the positive difference my subject made. And, most telling, 90 % of the room signed up to work with me further.

I laughed out loud. I was doing exactly what I help people stop doing – thinking they have to be like everyone else!

Do you ever have the reaction I did? When you notice that you do things differently, do you start thinking, "Uh-oh, I'm going to fail/get laughed at/do it wrong forever"?

Give yourself the gift of a reality check and realize that the people who make it big in the world are not mimicking other greats. Think of Stevie Nicks and her raspy voice – what if she had tried to be just like Joan Baez? Or if Joan Baez strove to be like Janice Joplin?

Instead of focusing on the sinking feeling that you're not up to par, focus on how your uniqueness lets you stand out from the crowd. Be yourself. You'll have more successes, and a lot more fun.

Lesson from a Bike Ride

I went for a bike ride and it was AWESOME.

I biked up a big hill, huffing and puffing, barely making it to the top. I enjoyed the view and, while biking down the hill, took my time so I wouldn't feel as though I was going to break my neck. I rode by a huge nursery I'd never noticed before, and even caught a glimpse of a bunny rabbit hopping across the road.

I felt so strong and capable and happy. So different from another recent bike ride where I felt weak, frustrated, and exhausted.

What was the difference? Comparison.

You see, on my energizing ride, I was on my own, creating my own experience based on my own strengths and goals.

The frustrating ride? I was riding with someone else with totally different strengths and goals. I compared myself to them the whole time, trying to keep up and feeling like I was falling short the entire time.

Think of it – two nearly identical bike rides, but one felt like a success and one felt like a failure.

Comparing myself to someone else changed my entire experience.

If you're feeling frustrated, I encourage you to check in with yourself, and see if any comparison is going on. Trust your abilities, forge your unique path to success, and enjoy the ride!

But Everyone is Doing It

Many years ago, I met a real estate agent at a training seminar. As we chatted, it became clear that she was really stuck in her business. Being a naturally curious gal, I started asking her questions about her marketing.

She told me that her primary marketing efforts focused on advertising, and she was spending $1,200 per month on it. I then asked about how many clients she got from her ads, and she said, "Oh, I don't get any clients from it."

Uh... ok. Bewildered, I asked one more question – "If you don't get any results, why do you spend so much on advertising?" She replied, "Well, I've always done it, and everyone else does it, so I have to do it."

I was speechless at the blatant absurdity of it. Spending over $14,000 per year on ZERO results?

(Other people's mistakes are so obvious, aren't they?)

Not so obvious is how we do this to ourselves – spending time and money on things that do not work, just because everyone else is doing it, and we've always done it. It's time to unearth the gunk that is draining your time, energy and money. It's easy. We'll use the real estate agent's statements as a guide.

1. "I've always done it." What do you do now that used to be effective, but no longer serves you or is totally out of step with the times?

2. "Everyone else does it." What strategies are assumed necessities in your industry or community, but aren't producing measurable results?
3. "I have to do it." What do you think you "should" be doing, but doesn't actually bring you any results?

Give yourself an honest evaluation, and remember that it's better to do nothing than to waste time and money on actions that have a proven track record of not working. Cut out what is wasting your time, and allow new, more effective solutions to emerge.

You Charge an Awful Lot

After giving a prospective client a proposal for my services, she said *"If I look at your pricing, and the actual hours of your time I get, well, it seems like you get paid an awful lot per hour!"*

Without missing a beat, we dove into her concerns and she agreed on the spot to become a client. My biggest client to date at that time.

As I hung up the phone, I thought, "WOW. A few years ago, her comment about my pricing would have totally freaked me out."

What did I say to close the deal? Well, first of all, let's travel back in time to how I would have responded earlier in my career. I would have started to justify or stammer or lower my prices (or all three) and it would have sounded something like this:

"Well uh, you see you have to understand that I, uh, work from home and, um have to pay for my own insurance and computer and taxes and I, you know, live in California where the cost of living is really high and, you know, I charge less than my competition, so you're really getting a deal actually but well, I guess, if you want me to give you my best deal, why don't we take another $1,500 off…"

Groan…

Now, compare that hot mess to how I responded this time:

"It's so interesting that you bring that up and there are two things going on here that are opportunities for us. The first has to do with us working together and the second has to do directly with your business.

First, I'm glad you brought this up so I can clarify everything you're getting in this program, and it goes way beyond the hours we spend directly working together. You will also get email access to review any documents or promotional materials you'd like feedback on. Your staff can also have access to me and be included in any of our sessions. In between scheduled sessions, if you need support through a specific challenge, you have access. What you're getting is a dedicated consultant so you can meet your goals faster, because you don't have to figure it all out yourself.

Which brings us to the second opportunity. Why aren't **you** charging more? If my prices seem high, I'm betting there is an opportunity in our work together to increase what you're charging. You're a 25-year expert running a million-dollar company – why aren't you charging more? That's one of the first things we should work on."

Feel free to use this as a model the next time a prospective client hints that you're charging too much for your expertise!

Acts of Boldness

I would say the majority of the people I work with would consider themselves non-conformists. After all, they are entrepreneurs!

But conformity isn't limited to all dressing the same, or agreeing about politics, or working at a 9 to 5 job. Conformity can be a very sneaky thing, and it can slowly eat away at what makes you brilliant and beautiful.

So how does this subtle conformity show up? It's at work behind the scenes when you –

- Don't clearly ask for what you really want
- Say yes to things that are unhealthy, stressful, or out of alignment with your vision
- Soften a position you believe in
- Lower your standards

This kind of conformity is all about trying to control other peoples' reactions. And the bad news is that it not only keeps others from really knowing you, it also distances you from your true, authentic self.

I absolutely believe in diplomacy, don't get me wrong. I'm not a fan of upsetting people for the sake of drama. That's definitely not what I'm talking about here.

I'm talking about boldness in the face of possible controversy or disagreement. The willingness to take a stand for what you feel in your heart is right – everything from simple things like getting your order right at a restaurant to deeper issues like politics and human rights.

This can be a scary proposition, I know. But it's also freeing. I challenge you to pay attention to how conformity shows up in your life, and commit acts of boldness every day!

About the Author

Mary Cravets is a Business Development Expert and Speaker who works with highly driven, busy entrepreneurs to significantly grow their businesses without working nights and weekends.

Her own entrepreneurial journey includes successes in real estate, networking events across the country and business consulting.

In the midst of these successes, Mary faced a combination of extreme financial and health crises which forced her to completely revamp her approach to business.

This new systematic approach resulted in tripling her income while cutting her work hours in half. She teaches audiences and clients the same systems she credits for her current success.

Mary lives on the beautiful central coast of California with her husband, Adam, and their cat, Annabelle.

For more inspiration, absurdity and strategy, visit www.MaryCravets.com.

Made in the USA
Middletown, DE
15 November 2020